HOSEA
Critic and Comforter for Today

I0957324

Let the word of Christ dwell in you richly as you teach and admonish one another with all wisdom, and as you sing psalms, hymns and spiritual songs with gratitude in your hearts to God. Colossians 3:16

By Rudolph F. Norden

Edited by Debb Andrus
Thomas J. Doyle, Series Editor

CPH.
SAINT LOUIS

Assitant to the editors: Cynthia Anderson

Copyright © 1996 Concordia Publishing House
3558 South Jefferson Avenue, St. Louis, MO 63118-3968
Manufactured in the United States of America

1 2 3 4 5 6 7 8 9 10   05 04 03 02 01 00 99 98 97 96

Contents

Why Hosea for Today?

In the Marc Connelly play *The Green Pastures*, in a scene set in heaven, the Lord inquires of the angel Gabriel who the man is who constantly passes His door, his figure casting a bent shadow on the celestial wall. Gabriel replies that it is the prophet Hosea, who desires God's compassion for a sinful people—the same divine mercy he experienced in his troubled life. And how did Hosea come to have such compassion? The reply is, "Through suffering." The prophet did suffer greatly, mostly because of his divinely directed marriage to an unfaithful wife. His suffering made him longsuffering.

Suffering, accompanied by patience, is not popular today. People try to avoid it, because they are told that it deprives them, in and out of marriage, of their loudly proclaimed personal rights, especially of their right to happiness. The experts often say, "Do you have trouble in your marriage? Don't let it interfere with good feelings. Get a divorce." Or if there is a problem at work, either factual or fancied, they say to walk away from the job and tell the boss to "shove it."

If suffering is encountered on any level of life, the temptation can be great to seek refuge in drugs and alcohol, because everyone is allegedly entitled to a day-long "happy hour." An alternative is to resort to lawsuits to recoup one's rights or to avenge wrongs.

What is there to do when one's professed Christian commitment threatens to bring on suffering? Is self-denial for the sake of Christ preferable to an easy surrender to the idols and icons of our time—to the mammon of materialism and the sex symbols of hedonism? The temptation is always present, also in Christendom of today, to make compromises with whatever the media trumpet as life's "highest good."

Enter the prophet Hosea, who is no stranger to suffering. He knows the high cost of unswerving loyalty to God. He is called to the task of being God's spokesman in an age of apostasy. He is willing to endure all the discomforts and unpleasantries connected with his life and calling: the unfaithfulness of his spouse, the ridicule of his enemies, the cold shoulder of friends. Now he enjoys high status in the sight of God, having entered it, as Gabriel supposedly says, "through suffering."

Hosea, as he himself would testify, gained eternal life through faith in the promised Messiah, the coming Savior. Hosea refers to Him as the new "David" (**3:5;** the original David was long dead), the "one leader" (**1:1**), under whom God's scattered people would be reunited. The events of Pentecost Day marked the beginning of that reunion as the Christian church. In bearing witness to Israel's covenant God, Hosea encountered the opposition of Baal worshipers, and these are identified as princes, priests, and people. He would agree with words later spoken by St. Paul, "I want to know Christ and the power of His resurrection and the fellowship of sharing in His sufferings" **(Philippians 3:10)**.

What is Hosea's message to his contemporaries and to us today? He is bold in telling his wayward generation that the scalpel of God's Law cuts deeply and sharply in order to remove the cancer of sin. He is even more eloquent—and his testimony more appealing—as he applies the Gospel of God's forgiving love. Here is one of his invitations: "Come, let us return to the LORD. He has torn us to pieces but He will heal us; He has injured us but He will bind up our wounds" **(6:1)**. Then, in what many Bible scholars take as a reference to the Messiah's resurrection as prefiguring and enabling our own rising from the dead, Hosea writes in the next verse: "After two days He will revive us; on the third day He will restore us, that we may live in His presence."

We find gems of Gospel truth in Hosea's prophecy. They constitute God's message to us today. The Word, both the Law and the Gospel, is addressed to us in these times. In Hosea's day, the great evil was idolatry, which Hosea calls spiritual adultery and which was symbolized by the unfaithfulness of Gomer, his wife. Nowadays we witness another kind of idolatry, with the true God all too often left out of the picture. What is the idolatry of our time? What shall we call the substitutes for God? Call one secular humanism, which is just a step away from atheism. As the people of our Western world become more and more post-Christian, they fall more easily into the trap of paganism with all the rites and wrongs it approves, even encourages. In Hosea's time there was "cursing, lying and murder, stealing and adultery ... bloodshed" **(4:2)**. Why this harvest of evil? The preceding verse gives the reason: "There is no faithfulness, no love, no acknowledgment of God in the land."

"Bloodshed follows bloodshed," Hosea laments **(4:2)**. The words have a familiar ring, as though taken right out of today's newspaper. What we have today is gang warfare and bloodshed in the streets. On the higher levels of society we find hubris (pride) and, further down, the raw manifestation of greed in gambling casinos and state lotteries.

Added to the breakdown of morals in civil life is the decline of true spiritual concerns in many parts of Christendom. What remains is mere religiosity: perfunctory ritualism and ceremonial observances "having a form of godliness but denying its power" **(2 Timothy 3:5)**. What is lost is the Gospel, which alone "is the power of God for the salvation of everyone who believes" **(Romans 1:16).** What many want in their churches is not the heritage of "old-time religion," but a modern "good-time religion," a watered-down "churchianity" of fun and games, a social fellowship with people instead of communion with the God of their salvation. In such a scheme of things, uncompromised faithfulness to Jesus Christ and suffering for His sake have no place.

Yes, we need Hosea's message today: God's own Word of grace and power will build us up. "Come, let us return to the LORD. He has torn us to pieces but He will heal us; He has injured us but He will bind up our wounds" **(Hosea 6:1).**

Part 1

Under the picture of marriage to an unfaithful wife, Hosea testifies to God's enduring love for faithless Israel.

Lesson 1

Hosea: God's Messenger (Hosea 1:1–9)

Theme Verse

The word of the LORD ... came to Hosea son of Beeri. **Hosea 1:1**

Goal

In this lesson, we will learn that the same word of the Lord that came to Hosea comes to us today. Although God is long-suffering and patient, He is just and must administer His judgment. To those who repent and turn to Him, rather than judging them as they justly deserve, God showers them with His free gift of forgiveness and salvation through Jesus.

What's Going On Here?

God spoke through His prophet Hosea using simple examples that should have been easy for the people to understand. Unfortunately, people's sinfulness gets in the way of understanding.

Hosea's relationship with his wife was a parallel of God's relationship with His people Israel. Hosea was always trying to win back his bride, just as God was always trying to win back Israel.

Hosea's message is pertinent to us today as we struggle with the temptations of a sinful world and our sinful flesh.

Searching the Scriptures

The opening verse, called the inscription, identifies the prophet by name, states his divine call, and indicates the time and place of his ministry.

The Man and His Mission (Hosea 1:1)

Read **Hosea 1:1.**

1. The name *Hosea* means "salvation." By his very name the prophet testifies to the lovingkindness of God. He enlarges on this theme throughout his book. Hosea is identified as "son of Beeri," of whom nothing is known. Why is a prophet's biography or personal data not as important as the content of his teaching?

See **1 Thessalonians 2:13.**

2. Hosea was a contemporary of Isaiah, Amos, and Micah. Listed as a "minor" prophet, he was, however, an important spokesman. Who are the "major" prophets? Why is there no difference as to the authority of major and minor prophets? See **2 Peter 1:21.**

3. Hosea's call to be a prophet came through a special divine revelation. How is this stated in the text? What was to be his first mission? Look ahead to **verse 2.** His marriage to an unfaithful wife was to symbolize the unfaithfulness of Israel to God.

4. Although no specific year or location is mentioned, the list of the kings of Judah and the naming of Jeroboam, king of Israel, place Hosea in the eighth century before Christ. Hosea addressed mainly the princes, priests, and people of the kingdom of Israel—the Northern Kingdom, also called Ephraim or Samaria.

Shalmaneser of Assyria invaded the land in 725 B.C. After a three-year siege, Samaria, the capital city of the Northern Kingdom, fell to the Assyrians in 722. The king of Assyria then carried the 10 tribes into captivity. The last king of Israel was Hoshea **(2 Kings 17:1–5),** who is not to be confused with Hosea the prophet. Why was Hosea's era a critical time for the Word of God to be preached?

The Man and His Marriage (Hosea 1:2–9)

The opening verse of this chapter stated that "the word of the LORD came to Hosea." The next verses tell us what message this word of the LORD contained. Hosea was to do something extraordinary. Read **Hosea 1:2–9.**

1. Hosea was to involve himself in a marriage to a woman prone to adultery. Some wonder how God could command one of His prophets to do such a thing. Remember that Hosea represents God, and Gomer represents God's people. What does God's command to Hosea imply about God's faithfulness even to a people prone to unfaithfulness? Compare this to Jesus' treatment of the divorced Samaritan woman **(John 4:1–26)** and the woman caught in adultery **(John 8:1–11).**

2. "Adulterous wife" stands for the people of Israel, who were unfaithful to God. What was the spiritual adultery Israel committed after God had entered into a covenant with them? To what false god(s) did they turn? Look ahead to **chapter 2, verses 8 and 13.**

3. The Lord told Hosea to name his son Jezreel. It was while in Jezreel that Jehu, a former king of Israel, had ordered the slaughter of the 70 sons of the house Ahab, whose heads he then put in two piles at the entrance to Jezreel **(2 Kings 10:1–11).** *Jezreel,* the name of Hosea's son, was to remind Israel that God would avenge this act of cruelty. Does God avenge cruelty and disobedience today? If so, how?

4. Read about the daughter named "Not Loved" in verses 6–7. The name in Hebrew, *Lo-Ruhamah*, means that God had suspended His love to Israel until such a time as the people returned to Him in faith. The kingdom of Israel would fall to the Assyrians, but what about the kingdom of Judah? How did God save Judah when Sennacherib's army invaded? See **2 Kings 19:35–36.**

5. The third child, a son, was to be called *Lo-Ammi*. What does the name mean? How do you think Hosea would have replied when people questioned him, "Why did you saddle your son with a name like that?" The covenant into which God had entered with Israel provided for this relationship: "I will … be your God, and you will be My people" **(Leviticus 26:12).** What, according to the name *Lo-Ammi*, would result if Israel persisted in its disobedience?

The Word for Us

1. The message of the prophet Hosea is not foreign to the readers of New Testament books. For example, compare **Hosea 6:6** with Jesus' words in **Matthew 9:13;** also **Hosea 13:14** with **1 Corinthians 15:54–55.** What do your findings say about the close union of the Old and the New Testaments? See **Hebrews 1:1–2.**

2. What's in a name? Sometimes very much, especially in biblical names. Hosea's name means "salvation." What is the meaning of the name *Jesus?* (See **Matthew 1:21.**) *Jesus* is the Greek form of the Hebrew *Joshua.* Does it make a difference what names we give to our children?

3. Pastors today receive their calls from God through congregations. The call is known as a "diploma of vocation." It is sent through the mail. How did Hosea receive his divine call? In what way may it have come to him? See **Hosea 12:10; Numbers 12:6;** and **Hebrews 1:1.**

4. The Word of the Lord still comes to us, as both Law and Gospel. How does it come? See **2 Timothy 3:15–17.** Discuss how God's Word, drawn from Holy Scripture, is conveyed to us in sermons, hymns, creeds and confessions, catechisms, admonitions and encouragements from fellow believers, absolution, tracts, and other Christian publications. How is the Word of God applied to us in Holy Baptism and Holy Communion?

5. Read **Isaiah 55:10–11.** Discuss how God's Word is a powerful, creative, redemptive, and sanctifying force. What is the chief content of God's Word? See **1 Timothy 1:15.**

6. For reasons hard for us to understand—and hard for us to reconcile with His holiness and love—God has at times commanded people to do difficult things: Hosea's marriage to Gomer; the command to Abraham to sacrifice His son Isaac; God's own Son sent to the cross **(Matthew 26:38–39).** Can you think of other instances? What about our own lives? What hard choices must we make to keep Christ first in our lives? See **Matthew 10:37–39.**

7. Ultimately, the outcome of events in history is not determined by military might—"not by bow, sword or battle, or by horses and horsemen" **(Hosea 1:7).** Today this military might would be defined as by planes, tanks, and "smart" bombs. History is God's story. God has the last word in

world affairs. What faith do believers confess in **Psalm 20:7?** What does this mean about threatening events in our time?

8. God is indeed a God of love and mercy. What reference do you find in **Hosea 1:7** to God's salvation? But God is also a God of justice. What overtones of divine judgment are to be found in the symbolic names of Hosea's children? How is God's justice plainly stated in **Exodus 20:5?** What is said in **Exodus 20:6** about God's love?

9. Hosea was willing to suffer, not only in his marriage but also because he sensed the spiritual downfall of his people. Summarize from Bible passages (**Matthew 5:10; Acts 14:22; Romans 8:17–21; Philippians 1:29;** and other texts) why Christians today must suffer at times, and to what end. Conclude by referring to Jesus' suffering **(Hebrews 5:7–10).** What good for us and all people came about through the suffering Jesus endured on the cross?

Closing

Pray together the following stanzas of "When I Suffer Pains and Losses."

When I suffer pains and losses,
Lord, be near, Let me hear
Comfort under crosses.
Point me, Father, to the heaven
Which Your Son For me won
When His life was given.

What at last does this world leave us
But a hand Full of sand
Or some loss to grieve us?
See what rich and noble graces
Our Lord shares With His heirs
In the heav'nly places.

Lesson 2

Reunited or Rebuked?
(Hosea 1:10–2:8)

Theme Verse

The people of Judah and the people Israel will be reunited. **Hosea 1:11**

Goal

This lesson will show how God goes after His children to bring them to repentance so that they might once again experience His love and mercy offered through the sacrifice of His only Son Jesus Christ.

What's Going On Here?

As we listen to God speaking through Hosea and other spokesmen, He may seem at times to be given to mood swings. In quick succession He threatens to punish evildoers, yet He promises grace and every blessing to the believers. He smites, yet He heals. As we proceed in our study of Hosea, we shall see that God is consistent. He threatens sinners in order to call them to repentance. This is the Law. All the while He is ready to forgive and bless all who through faith turn to Him. This is the Gospel. God's Word, as Law and Gospel, is consistent.

In the original Hebrew, Hosea wrote in poetry. The rhythmic cadences escape us in the translation. What remains, however, is the rich imagery of his writing. Many of the illustrative comparisons are taken from nature and everyday life. They depict Israel's sad spiritual conditions.

Searching the Scriptures

The Promise of a Reunion (Hosea 1:10–2:1)

Reread **Hosea 1:8–9** as background for today's lesson. Then continue this narrative by reading **Hosea 1:10–2:1.**

1. Read again the first sentence of **verse 10.** In what terms does Hosea speak of the numerical increase of God's people? Other prophets likewise speak of future multitudes streaming into God's kingdom with the dawn of the messianic age. See **Isaiah 49:18; 60:1–9.**

2. The second sentence of **verse 10** announces a changed designation of God's people, in keeping with their changed relationship to God. What is the new name? With God, new names are not just new labels; they bespeak the new life in Him. See **Revelation 3:12.** How is the *living* God different from *dead* idols?

3. **Verse 11** points to the messianic future. Read what it says. The prophet envisions the reunion of the people of the two kingdoms.

In Hosea's day Judah and Israel were separate kingdoms. They were never reunited—no geographical, political, or ethnic union ever took place. What is meant by the reunion of Israel and Judah?

God's Blockade (Hosea 2:2–8)

Through His holy prophets God admonished Israel, with whom He had entered into a covenant reminiscent of a marriage agreement. Not only Hosea but also Jeremiah used this illustration **(Jeremiah 3:6–14),** pointing out how God's people have been unfaithful to Him by practicing spiritual adultery by running after other gods. This unfaithfulness is personalized in Gomer, the faithless wife of Hosea.

1. In **Hosea 2:2,** what instruction did Hosea give his children with respect to their adulterous mother? With reference to Israel, who, besides the prophets, may have admonished the idolaters? Remember, there was a remnant of faithful believers. How many in Elijah's day had not worshiped Baal **(1 Kings 19:18)?**

2. Beginning in **verse 3,** Hosea points out what the consequences of persistent disobedience will be. On the blanks, indicate which verses declare

   a. the unfruitfulness and barrenness of sin; _____

   b. the withdrawal of God's love as a penalty; _____

   c. the unrealistic expectations people have of their false gods; _____

   d. the confinement in which sinners will find themselves; _____

   e. the futility of chasing after other gods. _____

3. **Verse 7** tells how the Israelites, pictured by Gomer, sometimes made short-term resolves to return to God, especially when things didn't go well. Why was this outward return not acceptable to God?

The Word for Us

1. The promise of great numbers in God's kingdom, "like the sand on the seashore," refers to the multitudes in God's spiritual Israel, the Christian church, made one in Christ, the seed of Abraham **(Galatians 3:16).** What was God's promise to Abraham **(Genesis 22:17–18)?**

2. The future reunion of God's people included the Gentiles. The reunion was marked by unity in Christ. Why is it important that reunion

efforts in Christendom today be based on full acceptance of Jesus Christ as the "one leader," as the one head of the church? Read what St. Paul says about this in **Ephesians 2:11–22; 4:5–6**. God is building His holy temple (the church) out of individual bricks (people) of various backgrounds. How are you a part of God's building program?

3. Some people are dubious about present-day emphasis on "church growth." Given the right motivation and approach, is there anything wrong with striving to increase the numbers in Christian congregations? With the use of a Bible concordance, check out the times when the book of **Acts** announces the growth of the church in numbers.

4. New Christians sometimes take biblical names when baptized. Referring to the names Hosea gave to his children (and to their new names given in **2:1**), can parents testify to their Christian faith by the names they give to their children? Note also that in **Romans 16** Paul mentions the names of many first-century Christians who retained their pagan names.

5. How do we proceed in rebuking members guilty of adultery, dishonesty, neglect of the means of grace, and the like? See **Matthew 18:15–19.**

6. Some today may identify with a church and make a profession of faith in the expectation that it will bring them earthly prosperity—like Gomer wanting food, drink, and clothing from her lovers. Apart from daily bread,

and all that this includes, has God promised us earthly riches? What may the faithful expect from God? See **Ephesians 1:3–10.**

7. Hosea threatened to cut off his love from Gomer's children **(2:4).** Under what conditions do children suffer with their parents? When not? See **Ezekiel 18:1–18.** An Old Testament saying was "The fathers eat sour grapes, and the children's teeth are set on edge." Children would say this when they sought an excuse for wrongdoing. Are there ways today in which children seek to avoid personal responsibility for their deeds by blaming their parents—their inherited genes, for example?

8. Regret by itself is not repentance, neither is "just feeling sorry." During Jesus' arrest, both Judas and Peter sinned. What was the difference between Judas' regret and Peter's repentance? See **Matthew 27:1–10** and **Mark 14:66–72.**

9. "I will block her path with thornbushes" **(Hosea 2:6).** How can God today keep sinners from further sinning? God also uses obstacles for other purposes. What was the experience of St. Paul on this score? See **Acts 16:6–10; 2 Corinthians 12:7–10.** What was the outcome?

10. Explain how for Christians the thornbush of God's disapproval becomes God's yes through the accursed tree of the cross. See **2 Corinthians 1:18–22.**

Closing

Pray together the words of this hymn:

I trust, O Christ, in You alone;
No earthly hope avails me.
You will not see me overthrown
When Satan's host assails me.
No human strength, no earthly pow'r
Can see me through the evil hour,
For You alone my strength renew.
I cry to You!
I trust, O Lord, Your promise true.

Lesson 3

The Price of Love
(Hosea 2:9–3:5)

Theme Verse

Love her as the LORD loves the Israelites. **Hosea 3:1**

Goal

In this lesson we will see that God is hurt when we turn away from Him. We will also see how He responds to our unfaithfulness with the Law—to show us our sin—and the Gospel—to show His love for us.

What's Going On Here?

In the rest of **chapter 2**—as throughout the book—the Lord, speaking through Hosea, alternates threats with promises. His purpose all along is to win Israel back as His people, the way a husband would put forth every effort to win back his deserting spouse. We are here given an insight into the heart of God, who wants all people to be saved through faith in Jesus Christ, His beloved Son.

In **chapter 3,** we see the continuing love of God for the faithless Israelites that runs like a golden thread throughout Hosea's prophecy. God will not abandon His chosen people, although they have abandoned Him and violated His covenant. In love He calls them to repentance. He wants to heal and to help. He is like a loving husband to an unloving spouse.

Searching the Scriptures
Betrayal and Betrothal (Hosea 2:9–23)

Read **Hosea 2:9–23.**

1. God at times punishes unrepentant sinners by withdrawing His blessings. He hopes to bring them to their senses. How does **verse 9** describe

this withdrawal? Remember: Gomer, who is to be deprived, stands for the people of Israel. What, apart from earthly blessings, did Israel stand to lose? See **Romans 9:3–5.**

2. The evil that people do is never hidden from God, and often it will be exposed before others. How did the Israelites make a spectacle of themselves before the nations with their Baal worship? Their idol could not save them. What befell Israel not many years later? See **2 Kings 17:1–23.**

3. Read **Hosea 2:11–13.** Besides worshiping Baal, the Israelites made a pretence of still observing the major festivals, new moons, and Sabbath days commanded in **Leviticus 23.** Why was God not pleased with these outward observances? Why is it not possible to serve the true God and idols? See **Isaiah 42:8.**

4. Read **Hosea 2:14–20.** God did not abandon His erring people but sought to win them back. In what vivid terms does Hosea describe this?

5. Read **Hosea 2:21–23.** Hosea uses picturesque language to declare the follow-through blessings of God on those who return to Him in faith. In a spiritual sense, they are blessed with peace, forgiveness, new life in Christ, and eternal life with Him in heaven. How does Jesus in **John 10:28** speak of the blessings of salvation? What meaning do the new names reflect? How do God's people respond to God's declaration, "You are My people"?

Love to the Unloving (Hosea 3)

Read **Hosea 3.**

1. Hosea is to prove to Gomer, his adulterous wife, what God wants to drive home to His people. What is God's instruction to Hosea? Review from the previous chapter **(2:5)** what the prophet's wife had done. What had she hoped to gain from other lovers?

2. Gomer, having in effect sold herself into the slavery of prostitution, was bought back. What price did Hosea pay for her redemption and restoration? Remember: The buying and selling of human beings was practiced in biblical times. See **Matthew 18:25.** Hosea's payment may be considered a dowry. What price did God pay for our redemption and restoration? See **Luke 23:44–46.**

3. What words in **Hosea 3:3** show that the prophet was to live as a loving husband with his wife? How was the redeemed wife to respond?

4. **Hosea 3:4–5** shows the application to Israel. The people of the Northern Kingdom were to be carried away into captivity in Assyria, and those of the Southern Kingdom into Babylon. Living in strange lands, they were to be deprived of their own government and of the free practice of their religion, whether that was worship of the true God or Canaanite worship. "Sacred stones" and "idols" were associated with pagan worship, while "sacrifice" and "ephod" were used both in the worship of the Lord and in Canaanite rites.

With the return of people from the Babylonian Captivity, the worship of the true God was restored under Ezra. By what name is the Messiah mentioned **(3:5)**? Refer to Peter's Pentecost sermon **(Acts 2:22–36)** to verify that Jesus the Messiah was meant here.

The Word for Us

1. The Bible, in many places, speaks of God's relationship (also Christ's relationship) to believers as that of a bridegroom and bride, of husband and wife. Why is betrothal and the promise of mutual faithfulness in marriage a fitting illustration of God's abiding love and loyalty? How does this blessed fact affect us? See **Ephesians 5:25–27** and **Revelation 21:2.**

2. God opposes every attempt to blend idolatry with the worship of Him as the true God. This is the sin of syncretism. Review what Paul teaches on the subject in **2 Corinthians 6:14–18.**

3. There is always a "door of hope" **(2:15)** in the lives of Christians no matter how adverse the conditions may be. What is the basis of our Christian hope? See **Psalm 42:5; Romans 8:22–39;** and **Hebrews 3:6; 6:19–20.**

4. In **Hosea 2:21–22** the Lord twice declares, "I will respond." Ordinarily we think of God as responding to our prayers **(Psalm 50:15)**. In what other ways does God respond as He makes known His holy and gracious will in Christ Jesus? How in nature? See **Matthew 5:45** and **Romans 1:18–21.** How in history? See **Acts 17:24–28.** How through the human conscience? See **Romans 2:12–16.** How through the written Law? See **Exodus 20:1–17.** How through the Gospel in Holy Scripture? See **John 3:16.**

5. The unremitting love of God for sinners is shown in the lives of many people. Hymn-writer William McComb lauds the love of Jesus, for it "found me when I sought Him not." From a hymnal read the spiritual song *Amazing Grace* and point out how John Newton testifies of God's love for him, "once an Infidel and Libertine, a servant of slavers in Africa," as stated on his epitaph. How has God asserted His saving grace in Christ Jesus in your own life?

6. Hosea's marriage to an unchaste wife was to symbolize God's enduring faithfulness to a faithless people. From this marriage, what do we learn from the prophet's own enduring love and concern for Gomer? What anguish must he have endured? Why should estranged marriage partners today go the extra mile to effect a reconciliation? How would they do this? For husbands, see **1 Peter 3:7; Colossians 3:19; and Ephesians 5:22–27.** For wives, see **Ephesians 5:22** and **1 Peter 3:1–6.**

7. Hosea redeemed his errant wife with a price: 15 shekels of silver and some grain. It was certainly more than a "cold cash" deal, since he was to "love her as the LORD loves the Israelites" **(Hosea 3:1).** Drawing the larger lesson from this, God loved us despite our sins, and "while we were still sinners, Christ died for us" **(Romans 5:8).** Discuss the length to which God went to redeem us from slavery to sin. Read **Matthew 20:28; 1 Peter 1:18; 1 Corinthians 6:20; 7:23.** What effect does God's boundless love and His extravagant purchasing price have on the faith and life of Christians?

Closing

Sing or pray together the following stanzas of William McComb's hymn "Chief of Sinners Though I Be."

Chief of sinners though I be,
Jesus shed His blood for me,
Died that I might live on high,
Lives that I might never die.
As the branch is to the vine,
I am His, and He is mine.

Oh, the height of Jesus' love,
Higher than the heav'ns above,
Deeper than the depths of sea,
Lasting as eternity!
Love that found me—wondrous thought—
Found me when I sought Him not.

Part 2

In a series of poetic discourses, Hosea alternates the Lord's stern
admonitions with tender promises of His forgiving love.

Lesson 4

An Unfaithful People
(Hosea 4:1–5:7)

Theme Verse

There is no faithfulness, no love, no acknowledgment of God in the land. **Hosea 4:1**

Goal

In this lesson we begin to study the charges that the Lord, through Hosea, made against Israel. We will discuss how these charges, made almost 3,000 years ago, are relevant for the world today, and what God has done to rescue people from slavery to sin.

What's Going On Here?

With **chapter 4** the second part of Hosea's prophecy begins. It consists of sermons or addresses in which Israel's sins are set forth in all severity, but which also let the light of God's forgiving love shine through like the sun in a clouded sky. It is generally believed that Hosea delivered these messages orally and later committed them to writing.

Searching the Scriptures
Sin Creates Shortages (Hosea 4)

Read **Hosea 4.**

1. Reread **verse 1.** The Lord, speaking through Hosea, brings many charges against His covenant people. He exposes the great spiritual and moral deficiencies among the people, as well as among the priests and prophets. What is missing? The first table of God's Law calls for the

acknowledgment of God as God and for full love to Him. What are the words of Jesus on this point? See **Matthew 22:34–40.** When faith in God and love for Him are lacking, unbelief sets in—and unbelief is the source of many other sins against God and people. See **John 3:18–21.**

2. What sins against God and people are mentioned in **verse 2,** and what is the result **(verse 3)?**

3. A sad situation prevails when the spiritual leaders in a nation are corrupt. Read **Hosea 4:4–9.** What accusations are made against priests and prophets? What is the result among people when the spiritual leaders fail to instruct them in the Word of God?

4. Read **Hosea 4:10–14.** The priests are a spiritual detriment not only for what they fail to do but also for what they do: they lead the people in the worship of idols. Why would idolatry be called spiritual adultery or prostitution? Refer back to **2:10–13.** Idolatry begets other sins, including real prostitution. How is this indicated in the text?

5. Read **Hosea 4:15–19.** Hosea's main concern at this point is to save whomever possible in the kingdom of Judah, where the Lord has preserved a faithful remnant of believers. Israel, also called Ephraim, was determined to revel in idolatry and its accompanying orgies: sex parties, drunkenness, and the like. Because it persisted in this, Hosea compares it to "a stubborn heifer"; an appropriate name, considering the people's worship of the golden calves set up by King Jeroboam I at Bethel and Dan. See

1 Kings 12:25–31. Bethel, meaning "house of God," Hosea called Beth Aven, "house of wickedness." What did the worship of golden calves mean to the Israelites?

God's Red Alert (Hosea 5:1–7)

Under the rule of King Jeroboam II, the times were relatively prosperous for the Israelites. But the abundance of God's temporal blessings did not prompt faithfulness to Him, the giver. In fact, the opposite was the case: the land of Israel (or Ephraim) was given over to idolatry, to the worship of Baal. This unfaithfulness to God, who had entered into a solemn covenant with Israel, is called spiritual adultery and prostitution by the prophet Hosea.

1. Read **Hosea 5:1–2.** Why were the priests taken to task? Refer back to **4:6–13**. How would God discipline the guilty parties?

2. Read **Hosea 5:3–6.** Not only the religious and political leaders but also the people are charged with idol worship and its accompanying evils. What misdeeds are mentioned? See also **4:2.** What evil thoughts and desires? What wrong attitudes? How would these sins cause the people to stumble? What change of heart must take place before they can truly approach God?

3. **Hosea 5:7** suggests that parents induce their children to sin by bringing them up in an atmosphere of idolatry. Further, not only individuals but a whole nation as such can induce other countries to copy its sins. What kingdom might thus be affected? See the last part of **5:5.**

The Word for Us

1. In **4:3,** Hosea speaks of animals, birds, and fish perishing as God's punishment of disobedient Israel. While the reference may be taken in a figurative sense here, it is true that other living creatures suffer because of the sins of people. See **Genesis 3:14–19** and **Romans 8:18–22.** We as human beings are entrusted with the care of the earth. What does this stewardship include? What measures for the conservation of endangered species do Christians support? "The earth is the LORD's, and everything in it" **(Psalm 24:1).** Why is a Christian's concern for nature different from that of secularists?

2. Instead of teaching and edifying the people, many priests and prophets of Hosea's time were ringleaders of idolatry. In what sense was greed their motivation? Read what Paul said about such leaders in **Romans 16:18** and **Philippians 3:19.** What may be special temptations for some clergymen today as they become TV celebrities? What appeal does materialism have for those whose "mind is on earthly things"? If possible discuss these questions with your pastor.

3. We may not know of people today who "consult a wooden idol and are answered by a stick of wood" **(Hosea 4:12).** But what forms of idolatry may tempt us here and now?

4. What was the role of goats, calves, bulls, and heifers in Old Testament sacrifices? See **Hebrews 9:11–14.** Why is it no longer necessary to shed the blood of these animals in the New Testament? See **Hebrews 10:1–14** and **1 John 1:7.**

5. The "New Moon festivals" of **Hosea 5:7,** held once a month, were pagan rites copied by the Israelites. They consisted in the worship of a creature instead of the Creator. See **Isaiah 1:13** and **Colossians 2:16.** Today many people worship things of nature, including the sun, moon, and stars. What is the difference between thanking God for things in nature and making them objects of worship?

6. Related to the above is the overall trend to secularism in our society. In some quarters it is marked by a return to paganism, as among the Israelites of Hosea's time. Granted that the distinction between church and state should be upheld, it is possible that the new secularism is meant to sidestep Christianity. How can Christians act as a leaven against such trends as taking Christ out of Christmas or turning Easter into a fashion show?

7. Hosea lived in a time when the majority of people, led by false prophets and priests, forsook the true God in favor of Baal. What do many people today regard as their highest good? Gomer's desires for food and water, wool and linen, oil and drink **(2:5)** typified Israel's desires for what they thought Baal had to offer. The Manicheans regarded all matter as evil. How do Christians regard material things? See **1 Timothy 6:17.** We sing, "Praise God from whom all blessings flow." What blessings? Why is God our highest good? See **Psalm 42:11; 73:25–26; 118:8.**

8. God's "red alert" of the Law calling people to repentance is not His last word. Compare the last verse in the Old Testament **(Malachi 4:6)** with that of the New Testament: "The grace of the Lord Jesus be with God's people. Amen" **(Revelation 22:21).** What does this mean to you?

Closing

In the midst of death, there is life. In the midst of sin, there is salvation through our Lord and Savior, Jesus Christ. Silently confess your sins to God. Then sing or pray together the following stanzas of "Jesus Sinners Will Receive."

> Jesus sinners will receive;
> May they all this saying ponder
> Who in sin's delusions live
> And from God and heaven wander!
> Here is hope for all who grieve:
> Jesus sinners will receive.
>
> We deserve but grief and shame,
> Yet His words, rich grace revealing,
> Pardon, peace, and life proclaim.
> Here our ills have perfect healing;
> We with humble hearts believe
> Jesus sinners will receive.

Lesson 5

The Sacrifice of Mercy
(Hosea 5:8–6:10)

Theme Verse

For I desire mercy, not sacrifice, and acknowledgment of God rather than burnt offerings. **Hosea 6:6**

Goal

In this lesson we will see how God's children rejected Him in Hosea's time and continue to do so today. We will also see that God is a faithful Father who sacrificed His only Son to save His children from destruction.

What's Going On Here?

In this section Hosea continues to pronounce woe on both the kingdom of Israel and the kingdom of Judah. Hosea's speech is graphic and vivid. It abounds in expressions that compare the people's wanton wickedness—and God's reaction to it—with situations in everyday life. These comparisons, introduced with "like," are short parables.

God the Father, like any good parent, longs for what is best for His children. But God's children, both in Hosea's time and today, are rebellious and disobedient and bring upon themselves destruction. God the Father sent His Son to pay for this disobedience and now desires that we show mercy to one another.

Searching the Scriptures
The Plague on Both Houses (Hosea 5:8–15)

1. Read **Hosea 5:8–9**. The sound of trumpets and battle cries heard in both kingdoms announce God's impending judgment. In what terms are

these predictions stated, and what is said to be the outcome? Beth Aven (or Bethel) was in Israel. Gibeah and Ramah were frontier towns in Judah.

2. The kings of Judah **(verse 10)** not only changed geographical boundary lines, but also, what is worse, they obliterated the distinctions between right and wrong. What would be the result of this?

3. The leaders of Israel **(verse 13)** in their distress sought an alliance with the Assyrian Empire. Why was this a tragic move? See **2 Kings 17:1–6.**

4. God expresses both His righteousness and His love **(Romans 2:4)** when He bids sinners to repent and return to Him. For how long—and to what end—does God wait patiently? **See 1 Peter 3:20; Hosea 5:15.**

5. Read **Hosea 5:12.** The moth is an insect that destroys crops and clothes. It stands for destruction wrought by sin. See also **Matthew 6:19** and **James 5:2**. Mounting moral rottenness, feeding on itself, can be a form of punishment. While moth and rot work quietly, another form of God's wrath can come with sudden violence. How is it sometimes poured out? See **Hosea 5:10** and **Revelation 16:1**.

A Standing Invitation (Hosea 6:1–10)

Many of God's gracious invitations begin with the word *come* (**Isaiah 55:1; Matthew 22:4; Revelation 22:17**). People are asked not only to approach Him but also to receive what He offers and to become a part of His family. Speaking for God, Hosea calls on the erring Israelites to come back into the family relationship with their heavenly Father.

1. The prophet's listeners needed healing and dressing of their wounds. Why were they torn to pieces at the hand of God? How would God heal them through the intervention of the Messiah? See **Isaiah 53:4–6.**

2. Salvation in Jesus Christ was foreshadowed. Where in Hosea's prophecy do we find such references?

3. St. Paul states that Christ died for our sins, was buried, and rose again "according to the [Old Testament] Scriptures" (**1 Corinthians 15:3–4**). Thanks to our Baptism into Jesus' name, "we have been united with Him … in His death [and] … in His resurrection" (**Romans 6:5**). Show from **Hosea 6:2** how believers pass from the sickness of sin, their bleeding state, and their spiritual death to new life.

4. Read **Hosea 6:3.** To "acknowledge" means not only to accept God's Word as true but also to confess one's faith in the Lord publicly. Jesus told Thomas to "stop doubting and believe" (**John 20:27**) and all His disciples to acknowledge Him before the world (**Luke 12:8**). Why is it not possible to keep our relationship to Christ a deep, dark secret?

5. Read **Hosea 6:4–10.** God's invitation to grace is constant. But people continue to sin, to relapse, to return to their old ways. The people of Ephraim and Judah had on occasion renewed their faith in God, but the commitment was not lasting. What does Hosea have to say about their alleged repentance? Describe God's resulting judgment.

6. **Hosea 6:6** is important in its own right, but also because Jesus quoted it **(Matthew 9:13; 12:7)** to show the priority of showing love over the mechanical performance of rites, ceremonies, and sacrifices. How do we worship God "in spirit and in truth" **(John 4:24)?** How in conformity with love to our neighbor **(Matthew 25:31–46)?**

The Word for Us

1. Hosea speaks of sin as bringing about "sickness" and "sores" **(5:13).** Sin is a spiritual malady and can also cause physical ailments. Doctors can help to heal the latter, but no human being can heal others, or self, from the sickness of sin **(Psalm 49:7–9).** Can the healing of mind and soul through faith in Christ's Gospel have a wholesome (and "wholistic") effect on one's physical health? If so, how?

2. **Hosea 5:15** suggests that God retreats from evildoers, not hearing their pleas for help as long as they remain impenitent. **Isaiah 54:7–8** says that at times God hides His face from us in anger for a moment, but adds, "With everlasting kindness I will have compassion on you." What truth should we keep in mind when it seems that God does not hear our prayers? How would you comfort and counsel someone who feels that God has deserted him or her?

3. How can "misery" **(5:15)** lead to a person's spiritual good? Draw your reply from Hosea. See also **Genesis 50:20** and **Romans 8:28.** What part has God played in your life to help you overcome grief?

4. God's Word consists of Law and Gospel. How do they differ? How did Hosea distinguish between the two? At times he proclaimed and applied the soothing balm of the Gospel. Why did he later on return to the Law? Should we today proclaim only the Gospel? Do we cheapen grace by preaching it to hardened sinners? What is the role of God's Law in our times?

5. God's promises in the Gospel are sure—"as surely as the sun rises" **(Hosea 6:3)**. We are to rely on them and be sure of our salvation in Christ. How does Hosea teach this? How is this taught throughout the rest of Holy Scripture? See also **John 1:16–17; Romans 5:20; 2 Corinthians 1:18–22; Titus 3:5–7**.

6. The sacrifices we bring—our gifts to missions, for example—are not a substitute for our love to God and people, but an expression of it. Under what circumstances can they become meaningless, even a sin? Recall the circumstances when Jesus quoted **Hosea 6:6** (see number 6 in the previous section).

7. Sin can be described in several ways—as error, trespass, transgression. When Adam sinned, he in effect broke his covenant with God **(Genesis 3:11; Hosea 6:7)**. Sin has a way of feeding on itself, of growing like a snowball. How do we by living persistently in sin break our baptismal covenant? How, instead, are we strengthened in Christian faith and life through our Baptism? See **Galatians 3:26–27; 1 Corinthians 6:11; 1 Peter 3:20–21.**

8. As Christians we don't want our love to be "like the morning mist, like the early dew that disappears" **(Hosea 6:4)**. List examples from Scripture of Christians building each other up through Word and sacrament. See **Acts 2:42; 20:7; 1 Corinthians 10:16–17; 11:26; 1 Thessalonians 5:11;** and **James 5:16.**

Closing

Encourage one another through prayer and/or song.

In Adam we have all been one,
One huge rebellious man;
We all have fled that evening voice
That sought us as we ran.

We fled our God, and, fleeing Him,
We lost our brother too;
Each singly sought and claimed his own;
Each man his brother slew.

But Your strong love, it sought us still
And sent Your only Son
That we might hear His shepherd's voice
And, hearing Him, be one.

O Savior, when we loved You not,
You loved and saved us all;
O great good shepherd of mankind,
Oh, hear us when we call.

Lesson 6

Longing for Repentance (Hosea 6:11–8:14)

Theme Verse

I long to redeem them but they speak lies against Me. **Hosea 7:13**

Goal

In this lesson we will study emotions: God's emotions when He sees the sinfulness and unrepentance of His people and our emotions as we struggle daily with our sin and are called by God to repent in order to receive the blessings of His forgiveness through Jesus Christ.

What's Going On Here?

God's longing for all sinners to be saved through faith in the redeeming merit of the Messiah has two important aspects. First, divine grace is the only reason for anyone's salvation, which is God's free gift entirely apart from good works **(Ephesians 2:8–9)**. Second, God's grace is universal; He wants all to be saved through the Gospel. It is often asked, "Why are not all saved?" Hosea continues to give the answer. God's " 'Yes' in Christ" **(2 Corinthians 1:20)** meets with people's negative response.

Hosea's charge of fine and gross idolatry against the Israelites runs like a scarlet thread throughout his prophecy. He likens it to adultery, to unfaithfulness to God. Fine idolatry consisted in the false trust that king and people put in military power—their own and that of the Assyrians. Gross idolatry was openly practiced in Baal worship and in the cult of the golden calves set up in Bethel and Dan **(1 Kings 12:25–33)**.

Searching the Scriptures
God's Yes, People's No (Hosea 6:11–7:16)

1. What does **Hosea 6:11–7:7** say about the certainty of God's exposure of sins and crimes? What evil deeds, matched by those reported in today's newspapers, are mentioned? What is said about the passions consuming king and people? At what occasions did these orgies take place?

2. Read **Hosea 7:8–11.** Israel, also called Ephraim, tried its hand at political alliances. Between which two empires did it alternate? At this game of international power, Israel was an amateur, committing foolish mistakes to it own disaster. Why is Ephraim compared with a dove? Why is it foolish for distressed people to forsake God and trust in people? See **Jeremiah 17:5.**

3. God's corrective dealings, if not heeded, will lead to destruction. In what graphic way is this described in **Hosea 7:12?**

4. All the while, God is still intent on the salvation of His covenant people. How is this fact declared in **Hosea 7:1** and **13?** What does Holy Scripture teach about God's universal grace toward a fallen world? See **Genesis 3:15; Exodus 34:6; John 3:16; 1 Timothy 2:3–4; 2 Peter 3:9.**

5. Read **Hosea 7:14–16.** Problems are not solved by tossing around on one's bed; warriors can't win with "a faulty bow." What do these comparisons tell us about the futility of sin?

Tarnish on the Golden Calf (Hosea 8)

1. Read **Hosea 8:1–3.** Israel's apostasy was so great that Hosea sounded a war cry against it. God would send an enemy—the Assyrians—with the swiftness of a ravaging eagle. The Israelites made a pretence of prayer. Why didn't God respond to their cries?

2. **Exodus 32:20** tells how Moses disposed of the golden calf Aaron had made in the wilderness: the people had to drink its ashes. All idols made by human craftsmen are given to vanity. Read **Hosea 8:4–6.** What were the people of Samaria to do with their "calf-idol"?

3. "They sow the wind and reap the whirlwind" **(8:7)** is a classic saying. Sin, starting as a gentle zephyr, can become a destructive tornado that leads to other sins **(Ephesians 5:3–7).** Point out from Hosea's prophecy what other sins accompany idolatry. Idolatry is also unproductive. In what agricultural terms does Hosea say this?

4. Read **Hosea 8:8–10.** The princes and people of Israel committed idolatry when they forsook God and trusted in armies. What resulted when Israel entered into an alliance with Assyria and other nations? In what way was Israel "like a wild donkey"?

5. Describe from **Hosea 8:11–14** the irony of bringing sin offerings when faith in the true God is lacking. Why is a faithless worship a sin adding to other sins? See also **Isaiah 29:13–14.**

The Word for Us

1. Some people seem to think they can get away with misdeeds and escape punishment so long as nobody finds out about them. Why can they not deceive God? See **Psalm 139:1–4.** Others endure sleepless nights **(Hosea 7:14)** because their consciences accuse them. How is peace with God attained? See **Romans 5:1–5.**

2. When the people of Israel forsook God and ignored the Ten Commandments, they lost the moral basis for everyday living. Then came this: "They practice deceit, thieves break into houses, bandits rob in the streets" **(Hosea 7:1)**. What should people today—citizens and governments—learn from this experience? How can Christians approach this problem?

3. Hosea speaks of drunkenness and sinful behavior at public celebrations such as "the day of the festival of our king" **(7:5)**. What present-day festivals are seen as an occasion for drunkenness and other sinful actions? How is Christian conduct described in **Romans 13:11–14?** What are some principles Christians can use to distinguish between joyful celebrations and sinful revelries?

4. Hot ovens were needed for the baking of bread. Hosea compares hearts filled with sinful emotions with heated ovens. Anger can be a smoldering passion that becomes a blaze **(Hosea 7:6–7)**. What does **James 1:19–21** have to say about unrighteous anger? What other human emotions can turn into burning passions?

5. What did God's covenant with Israel involve? See **Leviticus 26:9–13** and **Jeremiah 11:1–7.** How did the Israelites break it? Through Holy Baptism the triune God has entered into a covenant with us. What blessings does God convey through this sacrament? See **1 Peter 3:20–21.** How does faith in Christ's merits, imparted through Baptism, enable us to remain true to God? See **Romans 6:1–4.**

6. Whatever people regard as their highest good, that becomes their god. What can become the idols of people today? Money? Pleasures? Work? What about the many things (drugs, drink, etc.) to which people become addicted? Why do we need the Holy Spirit, working through the means of grace, to keep our whole selves—in body and in mind—as God's holy temples?

7. The Israelites under Moses were delivered from bondage in Egypt. Figuratively speaking, their sins marked a "return to Egypt" **(Hosea 8:13)** as self-imposed slavery. How do people in our times become their own worst enemies by returning to the bondage from which Christ has set them free? What is the personal slavery to which many return? How can they be rescued? See **Titus 3:4–8.**

8. The Israelites rendered lip service with their cry, "O our God, we acknowledge You!" **(Hosea 8:2).** Present-day believers sing praise to God in many forms. One canticle, the Te Deum, says, "We praise you, O God; we acknowledge You to be the Lord." Why does God hear us when we worship Him with expressions of praise? See **Ephesians 1:3–10.**

Closing

Pray together the following words of the hymn "As Surely as I Live, God Said."

As surely as I live, God said,
I would not see the sinner dead.
I want him turned from error's ways,
Repentant, living endless days.

All praise to You, O Christ, shall be
For absolution full and free,
In which You show Your richest grace;
From false indulgence guard our race.

Lesson 7

Adding Up the Sinfulness (Hosea 9–10)

Theme Verse

The days of reckoning are at hand. **Hosea 9:7**

Goal

In this lesson we will study the extent of God's justice. Hosea lists the sinfulness of Israel, but he may as well be listing our sins today. Even greater than God's justice is His mercy, evidenced in the person and work of His only Son Jesus, whom He sent to this world to redeem us from our sins.

What's Going On Here?

Sprinkled throughout **Hosea 9** are the names of places where Israel practiced idolatry and where God's judgment would descend on sinners. *Memphis* **(9:6)** was one of the chief cities of Egypt, thus to be buried by Memphis **(9:6)** was to be made slaves. *Gibeah* **(9:9)**, King Saul's place of residence in the land of Benjamin, had the disrepute of Sodom **(Judges 19:22–30)**. *Baal Peor* **(9:10)** was a site on Mount Peor where Baal was worshiped and where the Israelites, en route to the Holy Land, were lured into sexual immorality **(Numbers 25:1–5)**. *Gilgal* **(9:15)**, in the Jordan Valley, stood for pagan rites.

Many of the illustrations Hosea uses are taken from rural life. It is evident that most of his hearers and readers were engaged in agriculture, horticulture, and animal husbandry. In **chapter 10** Hosea refers to a "spreading vine," to "poisonous weeds in a plowed field," to "a trained heifer that loves to thresh." While Hosea's words penetrate to the depth of human depravity, they by no means rule out the mercy of God. The door of the heavenly Father's home is always open to those who return to Him in sincere repentance.

Searching the Scriptures
Time to Pay the Piper (Hosea 9)

1. Read **Hosea 9:1–4.** Before and during their exile in a foreign land the Israelites endured the penalties for their unfaithfulness to God. What futility would they experience in their worship exercises? How would they become spiritually contaminated?

2. **Hosea 9:5–9** shows the depth of Israel's moral and spiritual degradation in many ways, especially in its abusive treatment of the prophets. Hosea considered himself a spiritual watchman **(9:8)** on God's behalf. What does God expect of His watchmen and of the people they serve? See **Hebrews 13:17.**

3. **Hosea 9:10** tells how the Israelites, once a people giving promise of fruitfulness, became a disappointment to God when they turned to Baal worship. In what respect had they fallen from grace?

4. Persistent living in sin degrades people, causing them to become progressively more sinful and to be "as vile as the thing they loved" **(9:10).** How does **James 1:13–15** describe the growth of sin?

5. "The days of reckoning are at hand" **(9:7).** Sin demands its price; penalties follow wrongdoing. Divine punishment of sinners can take many forms. Sometimes it consists of letting evil take its course, sometimes of withholding good. Point out examples of both in **Hosea 9.**

Evil taking its course:

Good withheld:

6. God's declaration, "I will no longer love them" **(9:15)** implies that He formerly loved the Israelites and will renew His love when they repent. Where in the preceding chapters and verses did God declare outright His love and compassion? Also, look ahead to **Hosea 11:1.**

Sowing and Reaping with God's Blessing (Hosea 10)

1. Read **Hosea 10:1–15.** The children of Israel, having settled in the Promised Land, were off to a good start in serving the Lord. How is this indicated in the opening verse? But things went wrong. Israel, amidst its physical and spiritual well-being, turned its back on God and built stone altars for the worship of Baal. What divine judgment was sure to follow? See **Hosea 10:2.**

2. The idol worshipers, far from feeling secure, were beset by confusion and doubt. Their absence from the Lord brought no peace, only problems. How was pessimism, insecurity, and fear expressed in **Hosea 10:3?** Describe the disgrace and divine displeasure that followed, according to **verses 6–10** and **13–15.** The fulfillment is recorded in **2 Kings 17:1–6.**

3. There was still hope for Israel according to **10:12.** Hosea's earlier statement, "They sow the wind and reap the whirlwind" **(8:7),** has a counterpart in "Sow for yourselves righteousness, reap the fruit of unfailing love." If the Israelites, even at this late date, were to seek the Lord with sincerity and truth, they would be blessed with the fruit of God's love and with showers of righteousness. How did God's love bear fruit in the New Testament **(Galatians 5:22–25)?**

The Word for Us

1. Sin has its price. Pleasures and treasures seem to be in the offering, but they are a mirage. Instead the payoff is frustration and defeat. What are the ultimate wages that sinners earn? See **Romans 6:23.**

2. Sin has its price in family relations. It causes friction and sometimes an open battle **(Mark 13:12).** How does our reconciling Savior bring peace into marriages and homes? See **Ephesians 3:14–19.**

3. Sin and crime have their dreadful price in community living. Hosea says of sinners: "They practice deceit, thieves break into houses, bandits rob in the streets" **(7:1).** This is a vignette of our times. Apart from property losses, lives are endangered and lost. The Bible declares, "Righteous-

ness exalts a nation, but sin is a disgrace to any people" **(Proverbs 14:34)**. More than gun-control legislation is needed to control crime. What can Christians do to strengthen the moral foundations on which good government and citizenship rest? Look for hints in the cited **Proverbs** chapter. Also read **Romans 13:1–7**.

4. Sin has its price as far as our salvation is concerned. It cost the Son of God His life, so that through faith in Him we might be saved. This is the Gospel **(John 3:16)**. We are bought with a price **(1 Corinthians 6:20; 7:23)**. There is no "cheap grace." How does the truth of the high cost of our salvation affect—and effect—Christian living?

5. Does history repeat itself? Compare Hosea's words in the latter part of **10:8** with Jesus' words spoken on His way to Calvary **(Luke 23:30)**. Hosea foretold the attacks of the Assyrians, while Jesus, obviously quoting the prophet, referred to a later world power, the Romans. What horrors awaited Jerusalem under siege according to **Luke 19:41–44?** The strongest man-made fortress in the world cannot protect people from God's wrath. What is the only fortress that can protect us from God's judgment of our sins?

6. Have human beings in war situations become more humane? Compare the cruel killing of mothers and children at Beth Arbel **(Hosea 10:14)** with the fate of civilians in recent wars in Central America, Africa, Europe, and the Far East. Is there any difference? Is there such a thing as a "just war"?

7. Sowing in righteousness and then reaping the fruit of unfailing love is a good principle to follow in one's personal life. Most generally, people will respond in kind, that is, with kindness when love is shown. What did Jesus say on this point? See **Luke 6:38.**

Closing

Read **Psalm 46.** Then pray or sing the following stanzas of "A Mighty Fortress Is Our God."

> A mighty fortress is our God,
> A trusty shield and weapon;
> He helps us free from ev'ry need
> That hath us now o'ertaken.
> The old evil foe
> Now means deadly woe;
> Deep guile and great might
> Are his dread arms in fight;
> On earth is not his equal.
>
> With might of ours can naught be done,
> Soon were our loss effected;
> But for us fights the valiant One,
> Whom God Himself elected.
> Ask ye, Who is this?
> Jesus Christ it is,
> Of sabaoth Lord,
> And there's none other God;
> He holds the field forever.

Part 3

In an epilog Hosea renews his appeal to Israel to return to the Lord, adding the full assurance of His blessing.

Lesson 8

True Prophets
vs. False Profits
(Hosea 11–12)

Theme Verse

The LORD used a prophet to bring Israel up from Egypt, by a prophet He cared for him. **Hosea 12:13**

Goal

In this lesson we will learn of the love that God has for His children and the extremes to which He goes to show them His love. God's people ran from Him in search of happiness from the things of this world. God sent His prophets to call His people back into His circle of love.

What's Going On Here?

In **Hosea 11:1–11,** God, speaking through the prophet Hosea, assures the Israelites that His concern, compassion, and love are still in force. Although the persistently erring people deserved total rejection because of infidelity, God remained fully committed to His promises. Human love would have abandoned the sinners long before. But divine love is different. God, who is so superior to human beings, declares, "I am God, and not man" **(11:9).** He casts Himself in the role of a father who treats his children with patience and tender care.

Chapter 12, like the preceding ones, takes Israel to task for its corruption in all dimensions of life: spiritual, moral, social, economic, and political. The moral decay manifests itself in business practices—merchants defraud and use dishonest scales. Profits may lead to an outward prosperity in terms of shekels, but they bespeak moral bankruptcy. The claim to wealth is an idle boast, a nonnutritious delusion, for "Ephraim feeds on the wind" (12:1). There is no nourishment in that.

Searching the Scriptures

God's Love: The Tie That Binds (Hosea 11:1–11)

1. Read **Hosea 11:1–4.** How did God from the beginning—from its earliest "childhhood"—deal with His chosen nation? By what endearing name did He refer to them? How did He liberate, guide, and nurture them? How did the people respond to these acts of kindness?

2. **Hosea 11:5–7** describes the divine discipline God will exercise on an unrepentant people. In what ways did God permit Assyria to chastise Israel? True obedience is not expressed in cries of desperation but in turning to God with a believing heart. How is that stated in the text?

3. Read **Hosea 11:8–9.** In what respect does God demonstrate Himself as far superior to human beings? How is God compassionate with willful, persistent sinners? Is there a limit to His compassion?

4. A homecoming is foretold in **Hosea 11:10–11.** God's people, driven from their homeland, were in the Diaspora, that is, they were scattered among other nations. The biblical books of **Ezra** and **Nehemiah** tell about the return of various groups. How was this foretold by Hosea?

Prosperous but Perverse (Hosea 11:12–12:14)

1. Read **Hosea 11:12–12:6.** Both kingdoms, Ephraim and Judah, traced their origin to the patriarch Jacob, the father of Judah and grandfather of

Ephraim, one of Joseph's sons. Jacob was greedy. He contrived to receive Esau's birthright. He was called *Jacob*, which means "he grasps the heel." The name refers to Jacob's effort to get ahead of Esau, his twin brother, even as they were being born.

As for their descendants, the saying applies: Like father, like son—and like grandson. God willed that the people of both kingdoms would shun the evil example of Jacob but follow his good example. What right actions of Jacob are recalled in **12:4–6?** How was Jacob an example to his descendants, according to **verse 6?**

2. Look at **Hosea 12:7–8.** How did the merchants show their dishonesty? How did the deluded people of Ephraim express their self-righteousness, their carnal security?

3. Consider **Hosea 12:9–11.** How had God shown His love and power in the past? To what circumstances could He reduce Israel in later years? How did He communicate with His people?

4. Read **Hosea 12:12–14.** A parallelism between Jacob and Moses is pointed out: Jacob tended sheep to gain a wife **(Genesis 29:18),** and Moses tended God's people, hoping to present them to God as a pious spouse. Why did Hosea refer to Moses as a "prophet" **(12:13)?** In what words did Moses prophesy of the Messiah, the great prophet? See **Deuteronomy 18:15** and **Acts 7:37–38.** How did the Israelites react to God's care and concern?

The Word for Us

1. The Lord declares, "My heart is changed within Me; all My compassion is aroused" (11:8). How can this be harmonized with this statement: "I the LORD do not change" (Malachi 3:6)?

2. The words "out of Egypt I called My son" (Hosea 11:1) are quoted in Matthew 2:15, where they are applied to Jesus. This is appropriate, for Jesus, God's obedient Son, came into the world as the substitute for disobedient people in both the Old and the New Testaments. In what other ways does Jesus, as it were, retrace the steps of the Israelites to atone for their sins? For example, Israel spent 40 years in the wilderness, where Jesus also spent 40 days. Compare the following sets of references to contrast Jesus' obedience and reliance on God in the wilderness with Israel's disobedience and mistrust of God: Exodus 16:1–15; Deuteronomy 8:3 and Matthew 4:1–4; Exodus 17:1–7 and Matthew 4:5–7; Exodus 32:1–35 and Matthew 4:8–11.

3. Some people find it hard to harmonize God's love with His righteousness. Explain why no contradiction is involved. See 2 Corinthians 5:11–15.

4. There are times when the prayers of those who "call to the Most High" (Hosea 11:7) seem not to be heard by God. Recall Jesus' words in Matthew 7:21. Why didn't God answer King Saul's "prayers" any longer (1 Samuel 28:15)? Read what Isaiah 54:7–8 says about God hiding His face from us for a moment. Jesus on the cross was forsaken by God (Matthew 27:46). What assurance have we, thanks to Jesus' full atonement for our sins, that God hears our prayers and will not forsake us?

5. Hosea has stated many times that the Israelites did not follow through on their promise to repent and return to God in faith. What would you say to someone who postpones repentance because "God is always there for us" or "one can always repent on the deathbed"?

6. "Why spend money on what is not bread," Isaiah (55:2) asks. Hosea declares that "Ephraim feeds on the wind" (12:1). What is worse, it relies on the hot east wind that blows out of the Arabian desert and burns everything. These texts have spiritual implications. Many claims are made for "new religions" or a "new age." In most cases these "new" religions and philosophies are a rehash of ancient beliefs. Have you encountered any of these? Are they spiritually nourishing? See 2 Peter 2.

7. A threefold formula of faith and piety is stated in Hosea 12:6: "You must return to your God; maintain love and justice, and wait for your God always." Three steps are indicated: (1) turning to God in sincere repentance and in the renewal of faith in Christ; (2) living a life of love and justice; and (3) waiting for God to answer our prayers, fully expecting that He will keep all His promises. Scripture interprets Scripture. How do the following passages substantiate the above truths: Mark 1:14–15; Micah 6:8; Romans 8:22–25?

8. Dishonesty in business is a matter not only between seller and buyer: God is the third party in these relationships (Leviticus 19:35–36). Why should Christian merchants who take to heart 1 Thessalonians 4:6, "no one should wrong his brother or take advantage of him," do so out of love rather than fear? See Matthew 22:39. Why out of love for Christ? See 1 Peter 1:18–19.

9. God once dealt with His people by speaking to and through the prophets, including Moses. Would you believe a person who claims that God had given him or her a special revelation directly? See **Hebrews 1:1–4.** How does one check on the claimed orthodoxy of modern prophets? See **Acts 17:11** and **1 John 4:1.**

Closing

The true wealth of the world rests in God's Word. Sing or pray together these stanzas from the hymn "Thy Strong Word."

Lo, on those who dwelt in darkness,
Dark as night and deep as death,
Broke the light of Thy salvation,
Breathed Thine own life-giving breath.
Alleluia, alleluia! Praise to Thee who light dost send!
Alleluia, alleluia! Alleluia without end!

Thy strong Word bespeaks us righteous;
Bright with Thine own holiness,
Glorious now, we press toward glory,
And our lives our hopes confess.
Alleluia, alleluia! Praise to Thee who light dost send!
Alleluia, alleluia! Alleluia without end!

Lesson 9

The King's Edict
(Hosea 13)

Theme Verse

You shall acknowledge no God but Me, no Savior except Me. I cared for you in the desert. **Hosea 13:4–5**

Goal

In this lesson we will learn that God, our heavenly King, has provided us with all we need for this life and the next. Out of thanks, we worship and praise Him. In the past, sin has skewed the worship practices of God's people and He has had to discipline them. Use this lesson to evaluate your worship and your life: Are they centered in service to the King of kings?

What's Going On Here?

We confess in the Nicene Creed: "I believe in one God ..." This is biblical, for Moses has written, "Hear, O Israel: The LORD our God, the LORD is one" **(Deuteronomy 6:4)**. Through Hosea He declares, "You shall acknowledge no God but Me" **(13:4)**. God is also the one and only Savior. For the salvation of all He sent His Son into the world, of whom St. Paul declares, "There is but one Lord, Jesus Christ, through whom all things came and through whom we live" **(1 Corinthians 8:6)**. Further, God's people are one in Christ, as our Lord states, "There shall be one flock and one shepherd" **(John 10:16)**.

Not only were the people having problems with idols, they also had a misunderstanding as to the role of a king. Long ago, in the days when judges ruled the people, the elders of Israel came to Samuel and said, "Appoint a king to lead us, such as all the other nations have" **(1 Samuel 8:5)**. The Lord told Samuel to give them a king. A man named Saul, described as "an impressive young man" **(1 Samuel 9:2)**, was appointed as the first king.

The people had wanted a king "to go out before us and fight our battles" (**1 Samuel 8:20**). In his prophecy Hosea recalls this event.

Searching the Scriptures

One God, One Savior, One People (Hosea 13:1–8)

1. Read **Hosea 13:1–3.** Describe the widespread practice of gross idolatry, its dreadful inclusions, its utter vanity. How did the images of Baal come into being? What horrible sacrifices were performed, causing the people to "sin more and more"? How was false affection demonstrated? In what everyday expressions is the vanity of pagan rites—and the vain outcome of those who practice them—declared?

2. Look over **Hosea 13:4–8** and show the contrast between a man-made idol and the true God. What is the force of the word *your* in the designation "your God"? What does it imply concerning the covenant with God? See **Exodus 6:2–9.** How did the true God demonstrate His power, concern, and kindness to Israel of old? How did they, especially the people of Hosea's time, respond to God's love? What was the threatened result of the sin of unbelief?

3. Read again **Hosea 13:4–8.** God declares Himself to be the only Savior of His people. Above and beyond Israel's earthly deliverance, spiritual salvation was offered. Moses and the prophets testified of the coming Savior, the Messiah. Cite some of these prophecies.

4. God did not lead several Israels out of Egypt but only one. He wanted them to be and remain one people. How is the New Testament church a fulfillment of God's saving purpose? See **1 Peter 2:9–10.**

From Death to Life (Hosea 13:9–16)

1. Read **Hosea 13:9–10.** The king and all his successors could not save the people from ruin. What was worse, many of the kings and princes were the ringleaders of ungodliness. What action did the Lord take in the end?

2. Read **Hosea 13:12–13.** In what words did Hosea say that Israel's sins were not to be lightly dismissed? The birth of a child has its price: It costs the mother much pain, as also Jesus declared **(John 16:21).** Every child should remain mindful of this and lead a life giving honor to his or her mother. The Israelites, however, did not appreciate what God had done to bring them into existence. What had God done? Refer back to **Hosea 13:4–6.** In what respect did the people show a lack of wisdom?

3. Read **Hosea 13:14.** God puts Himself on record as good and gracious to all who repent and believe in His Son as the Savior. His purpose is ever the same: He wants people to come to the knowledge of the truth and be saved **(1 Timothy 2:4; 2 Peter 3:9).** The Son of God became man in order "to serve, and to give His life as a ransom for many" **(Matthew 20:28).** The hymn lines say *from* what and *for* what Christ redeemed us: "Blest the children of our God, They are bought with Christ's own blood; They are ransomed from the grave, Life eternal they will have." Cite once more the magnificent words of Hosea in which God proclaims Christ's redemption of us from sin and His triumph over death. Refer to St. Paul's use of Hosea's words as he bases our resurrection from the dead on Christ's resurrection **(1 Corinthians 15:55–57).**

4. It comes as a shock in **Hosea 13:14b–16** that so soon after the promise of ransom and redemption the Lord declares, "I will have no compassion." Why this announcement? What have the people of Samaria

(Ephraim, the kingdom of Israel) done to thwart God's mercy? In what words does Hosea announce God's redemptive purpose?

The Word for Us

1. Man-made idols are cited in the Bible not only as helpless gods but also as objects of ridicule and sarcasm. See **Psalm 115:1–8.** Note the punch line: Idols are silly and lifeless, and so are "those who make them … and … trust in them." Note also that this caricature of pagan gods was given to ridicule other *people* and *things* made by people as their god, their highest good. What other people and what things? See **Psalm 118:9; Matthew 10:37–39; Philippians 3:19.**

2. About human sacrifices: We may not be aware of human sacrifices brought by people nowadays, although instances of it among primitive peoples are occasionally reported. In what ways, apart from rituals on pagan altars, are human beings still being "sacrificed"? What idol or false god do people create when they place their ego or personal convenience above the will of God?

3. To "kiss the calf-idols" seems a degrading act of idol worship. Why is this misplaced affection? Whom should we love above everything else? How do we, in spirit and in truth, show our love for Christ? See **John 14:23.** How in our attitude to those in need? See **Matthew 25:31–46.**

4. "I cared for you in the desert. ... I fed them" **(Hosea 13:5–6).** Discuss how God provides for us in our daily living. We receive no manna from heaven. What does God give us?

5. It is important that we elect the best people available for official positions on all levels of government. But what are our rulers unable to do for us? What may we rightfully expect of them? How does Hosea teach us not to regard high officials as almighty gods **(13:10–11)?**

6. The prophet tells Ephraim that its guilt "is stored up" and that its sins are "kept on record" **(13:12).** When does God clean the slate, erase and forgive sin and guilt? Discuss this in the light of **Colossians 2:13–15.**

7. If death and the power of the grave are conquered, why do people still die? See **Genesis 2:15–17** and **Romans 6:12–17.** Temporal death remains, but why does it hold no terror for Christians? See **Hebrews 2:14–16.**

Closing

Sing or pray together the hymn "Blest the Children of Our God."

Blest the children of our God,
They are bought with Christ's own blood;
They are ransomed from the grave,
Life eternal they will have:
With them numbered may we be
Here and in eternity!

They are justified by grace,
They enjoy the Savior's peace;
All their sins are washed away,
They will stand in God's great day:
With them numbered may we be
Here and in eternity!

They are lights upon the earth,
Children of a heav'nly birth;
One with God, with Jesus one;
Glory is in them begun:
With them numbered may we be
Here and in eternity!

Lesson 10

Return to the Lord
(Hosea 14; Review of Hosea)

Theme Verse

Return, O Israel, to the LORD your God. ... I will heal their waywardness and love them freely. **Hosea 14:1, 4**

Goal

This lesson will conclude our study of Hosea. In the last chapter, Hosea again recounts the blessings offered by God to His repentant children. An overall review of the book shows this same theme to be prevalent throughout.

What's Going On Here?

Hosea has spoken words of sharp rebuke in calling the idolatry-prone Israelites to a life of repentance. His purpose all the while was constructive. Invitations followed invectives. The people were assured that God desired their salvation. If they changed their ways, He would renew them in the grace of the atoning Messiah, the Christ. Many years later, when the time of fulfillment had come, St. Peter preached in the home of the centurion Cornelius: "All the prophets testify about Him that everyone who believes in Him receives forgiveness of sins through His name" **(Acts 10:43)**. This is also what Hosea proclaimed when he foretold the true Israelites' reunion of faith in "David their king" **(3:5),** a clear reference to Him who was both David's son and Lord, the Messiah.

Many truths, applicable to our own lives, are revealed in Hosea's prophecy. Of course, times and living conditions have changed since Hosea's era almost 3,000 years ago, but human nature is still the same. The basic problems of the human race remain. Above all, God is still the same: just and righteous, gracious and merciful. Along with the entire Old Testament

Scriptures, Hosea's writing teaches us "so that through endurance and the encouragement of the Scriptures we might have hope" **(Romans 15:4).**

Searching the Scriptures
A Plea and a Pledge (Hosea 14)

1. In **14:1–2** Hosea tells the people what words to take with them as they returned to God. What were they to say? Their purpose—and the desired outcome—was to be a people of faith and to bear fruit to God's glory. What is the fruit of faith manifested in a sanctified life? See **Galatians 5:22–26.** What is the fruit of our lips? See **Psalm 63:1–5.**

2. **Hosea 14:3** rules out the Israelites' faith in the Assyrians, in their own military cavalry, and in man-made idols. How were they to confess trust in the goodness of God?

3. Read **Hosea 14:4–8.** What is the Lord's declaration to Israel if they return to Him? Read **Psalm 103:8–14.** For whose sake does God forgive sinners? See **Isaiah 53:5** and **2 Corinthians 5:16–21.** God blesses abundantly all those who are His own and live under Him in His kingdom. In what picture language, taken from nature, are these blessings described **(Hosea 14:5–8)?**

4. **Hosea 14:9** describes idol worship as utmost folly, but faith in the God of salvation as the highest wisdom. How are we made wise unto salvation? See **2 Timothy 3:15–16.** How does one walk in God's ways? See **Deuteronomy 10:12–13.** How are God's people motivated and enabled to do good works? See **Ephesians 2:8–10; Philippians 2:13.**

Hosea's Prophecy in Review

1. The prophet's first revelation from God in **chapter 1** was hard to accept: he was to marry a woman who proved unfaithful. Hosea's wife, Gomer, symbolized the people of Israel, who committed spiritual adultery by worshiping Baal and the golden calves. How did this marriage bring grief and suffering to Hosea? It is most unlikely that God will give a similar assignment to any of us. But He may call on us to do difficult things, to make hard choices. What was Abraham to do? See **Genesis 22:1–2.** Moses? See **Exodus 3:10.** St. Paul? See **Acts 9:15–16.** Motivated by God's love for us in Christ Jesus, how can we respond when God confronts us with difficult tasks?

2. In his severe castigation of sin and in his witness to salvation in the coming Messiah, Hosea stands shoulder to shoulder with his contemporaries. Their agreement is most remarkable. Compare **Hosea 3:5** with **Isaiah 2:2** and **Micah 4:1; Hosea 13:14** with **Isaiah 25:7–8; Hosea 14:8** with **Daniel 4:10–12, 22.** How can we account for this unity in the prophets' testimonies?

3. God deals righteously with sinners. His Law rebukes them and calls them to unconditional repentance. He declares through Hosea: "Because you have rejected knowledge, I also reject you" **(4:6).** Cite other instances of God's warning message in Hosea.

4. God is pictured as extending His hands and pleading with the rebellious people to return to His family. Where in Hosea's prophecy were such invitations extended? How are they similar to the father's love in Jesus' parable of the lost son **(Luke 15:11–32)?** What does this tell us about God as our waiting Father today?

5. Read these passages from Hosea again, and describe in your own words the Gospel promises they contain: **1:10–11; 2:14–15; 3:1; 6:1–3; 11:1; 13:14; 14:2.**

The Word for Us

1. What are some present-day efforts to secularize, that is, exclude God, from everyday life? What about things like the removal of manger scenes from the public square at Christmas time? Compare Hosea's call to exercise true wisdom with the current trend of secular humanism. Which way shall we go?

2. Much of Hosea's prophecy was written in rhythmic speech, in vivid poetry. Figures of speech abound. There is a saying, "Biblical poetry should not be made to 'walk on all fours' " that is, literalism is to be avoided when the text is poetic. For example, when Isaiah declares that "all the trees of the field will clap their hands" **(55:12)**, he does not wish to say that trees have hands and can clap. The point is *joy*. Select several expressions from **Hosea 14** (for example, "fragrance like a cedar of Lebanon") and say what truth is expressed in such poetry. Another temptation to be avoided: Taking factual, nonfigurative statements of the Bible and dismissing them as "just poetry."

3. Some people think that Christianity is for losers—that it is both futile and foolish to be a Christian. What is really folly? See **Psalm 14:1.** What is true wisdom? See **Ephesians 3:14–19.**

4. The idol Baal as such is no longer a threat, but what forms of gross and fine idolatry prevail today? The Israelites tried to blend Baal worship with their own feast days. Nowadays the attempted fusion of true and false religion results in a Christianity-plus formula: salvation by faith *plus* good works. Why does this plus-formula not work? See **Romans 3:27–28; 1 Corinthians 5:6–8;** and **Galatians 1:6–9.**

5. **Hosea 6:6,** "I desire mercy, not sacrifice," has to be taken seriously, for Jesus quoted these words several times. What do these words tell us about empty ritualism in our day?

6. Renewal in the Gospel: Through Hosea God invited His people to return to Him penitently to receive the forgiveness of their sins through faith in the atoning Messiah and to receive strength for holy living. This is wisdom of the highest kind. The prophet asks at the end: "Who is wise? He will realize these things. Who is discerning? He will understand them. The ways of the LORD are right; the righteous walk in them" **(14:9).** Make it your daily prayer that God grant you this renewal in the Gospel!

Closing

Close this last lesson by singing or praying these stanzas of the hymn "Take My Life, O Lord, Renew":

> Take my life, O Lord, renew,
> Consecrate my heart to You;
> Take my moments and my days;
> Let them sing your ceaseless praise.

Make my will Your holy shrine,
It shall be no longer mine.
Take my heart, it is Your own;
It shall be Your royal throne.

Take my love, my Lord, I pour
At Your feet its treasure store;
Take my self, Lord, let me be
Yours alone eternally.

HOSEA
Critic and Comforter for Today

Leaders Notes

Preparing to Teach Hosea

In preparation to teach, consult introductions to the book of Hosea (such as the one in the Concordia Self Study Bible), and if possible read the People's Bible Commentary on *Hosea, Joel, Amos* available from Concordia Publishing House.

Also read the text in a modern translation. The NIV is generally referred to in the lesson comments. The NIV shows clear paragraph divisions, the structure of the book, and the poetic form in which almost all of Hosea is written.

In the section "Searching the Scriptures," the leader serves as a guide using the questions given (or others) to help the class discover what the text actually says. This is a major part of teaching, namely, directing the learners to discover for themselves. Another major portion of each lesson is helping the student by discussion to see the meaning for our times, for church and world today, and especially for our own lives.

Group Bible Study

Group Bible study means mutual learning from one another under the guidance of a leader or facilitator. The Bible is an inexhaustible resource. No one person can discover all it has to offer. In a class many eyes see many things and can apply them to many life situations. The leader should resist the temptation to "give the answers" and so act as an "authority." This teaching approach stifles participation by individual members and can actually hamper learning. As a general rule the teacher is not to "give interpretation" but to "develop interpreters." Of course there are times when the leader should and must share insights and information gained by his or her own deeper research. The ideal class is one in which the leader guides class members through the lesson and engages them in meaningful sharing and discussion at all points, leading them to a summary of the lesson at the close. As a general rule, don't tell what the learners can discover by themselves.

Have a chalkboard and chalk or newsprint and marker available to lead significant points of the lesson. Rephrase your inquiries or the inquiries of participants as questions, problems, or issues. This provokes thought. Keep discussion to the point. List on the chalkboard or newsprint the answers given. Then determine the most vital points made in the discussion. Ask additional questions to fill apparent gaps.

The general aim of every Bible study is to help people grow spiritually, not merely in biblical and theological knowledge, but also in Christian thinking and living. This means growth in Christian attitudes, insights, and skills for Christian living. The focus of this course must be the church and the world of our day. The guiding question will be, What does the Lord teach us for life today through the book of His prophet Hosea?

Teaching the Old Testament

Teaching an Old Testament book first spoken and written for ancient Israel can become just an ancient history if it is not applied to life in our times. The leader needs to understand the time and culture in which the book was written. He or she needs to understand the historical situation of the divided kingdom (Judah and Israel) and the "secularization" of life. We too, perhaps more than they, are exposed to a secularization of life in which we forget that we are God's people and have a Christian mission. We live in what some historians call a "post Christian" culture. How will we recall God's people to live under God's covenant? to accept themselves as having the priesthood through which God will build His kingdom? How can we help our people get a better "image" of themselves as God's people in the sense of **1 Peter 2:1–10?**

Teaching the Old Testament can degenerate into mere moralizing, in which do-goodism becomes a substitute for the Gospel and sanctification gets confused with justification. Actually the justified sinner is not moved by Law but by God's grace to a totally new life. His or her faith is always at work for Christ in every context of life. Meaningful personal Christianity consists in a loving trust in God that is evidenced in love for one's fellows. Having experienced God's free grace and forgiveness, the Christian daily works in his or her world to reflect the will of God for humanity in every area of human endeavor.

The Christian leader is Gospel oriented, not Law oriented. He or she distinguishes Law from Gospel. Both are needed. There is no clear Gospel unless we first have been crushed by the Law and see our sinfulness. There is no genuine Christianity where faith is not followed by life pleasing to God. In fact, genuine faith is inseparable from life. The Gospel alone gives us the new heart that causes us to love God and our neighbor.

When Christians teach the Old Testament, they do not teach it as a "lawbook," but instead as books containing both Law and Gospel. They see the God of the Old Testament as a God of grace who out of love establishes a covenant of mercy with His people **(Deut. 7:6–9)** and forgives their sins. Christians interpret the Old Testament using the New Testament message of fulfilled prophecy through Jesus Christ. They teach as leaders who personally know the Lord Jesus Christ as Savior, the victorious Christ who gives all believers a new life **(2 Cor. 5:17)** and a new mission **(John 20:21).**

Pace Your Teaching

Do not try to cover every question in each lesson. This attempt would lead to undue haste and frustration. Be selective. Pace your teaching. Spend no more than five minutes with "Theme Verse" and "Goal" and two or three minutes with "What's Going On Here?" Take time to go into the text paragraph by paragraph, but not verse by verse or word by word. Get the sweep of meaning. Occasionally stop to help the class gain understanding of a word or concept. Allow 20 minutes to apply the lesson ("The Word for Us") and five minutes for "Closing." This schedule, you will notice, allows only about 30 minutes for working with the text ("Searching the Scriptures").

Should your group have more than a one-hour class period, you can take it more leisurely. But do not allow any lesson to "drag" and become tiresome. Keep it moving. Keep it alive. Keep it deeply meaningful. Eliminate some questions and restrict yourself to those questions most meaningful to the members of the class. If most members study the text at home, they can report their findings, and the time gained can be applied to relating the lesson to life.

Good Preparation

Good preparation by the leader usually affects the pleasure and satisfaction the class will experience. Purchase at least one of the shorter commentaries to aid in your personal preparation. See the list of references for suggested books.

Suggestions to the Leader for Using the Study Guide

The Lesson Pattern

This set of 10 lessons is based on a significant and timely Old Testament writing—the book of Hosea. The material is designed to aid *Bible study*, that is, to a consideration of the written Word of God, with discussion and personal application growing out of the text at hand. The typical lesson is divided into six sections:

1. "Theme Verse"
2. "Goal"
3. "What's Going On Here?"
4. "Searching the Scriptures"
5. "The Word for Us"
6. "Closing"

"Theme Verse" and "Goal" give the leader assistance in arousing the interest of the group in the concepts of the chapter. Current events and conditions are cited to "warm up" the class and convince its members that the Word of God spoken through Hosea is relevant to their present situation. Here the leader stimulates minds. Do not linger too long over the introductory remarks. You merely show that the chapter to be studied is most meaningful to Christian faith and life today.

"What's Going On Here?" helps you gain an understanding of the textual portion to be considered in the session. Before the text is broken down for closer scrutiny, it should be seen in the perspective of a greater whole. At this point the class leader takes the participants to a higher elevation to show them the general layout of the lesson. This overview gives the group an idea where it is going, what individual places are to be visited, and how the two are interrelated.

"Searching the Scriptures" provides the real "spadework" necessary for Bible study. Here the class digs, uncovers, and discovers; it gets the facts and observes them. Comment from the leader is needed only to the extent that it helps the group understand the text. The same is true of looking up the indicated parallel passages. The questions in the study guide, arranged under subheadings and corresponding to sections within the text, are intended to help the learners discover the meaning of the text.

Having determined what the text says, the class is ready to apply the message. Having heard, read, marked, and learned the Word of God, we proceed to digest it inwardly through discussion, evaluation, and application. This is done, as the study guide suggests, by taking the truths of Hosea and applying them to the world and Christianity in general and then to personal Christian life. Class time will not permit discussion of all questions and topics. In preparation the leader will select two or three and focus on them. Be sure to include questions from the "on a more personal level" category, since they bring God's message to the individual Christian. Close the session by reviewing one important truth from the lesson.

Remember, the Word of God is sacred, but the study guide is not. The guide offers only suggestions. The leader should not hesitate to alter the guidelines or substitute others to meet his or her needs and the needs of the participants. Adapt your teaching plan to your class and your class period. The first lesson suggests more presentation by the leader since it is introductory. Good teaching directs the learner to discover for himself or herself. For the teacher this means directing the learner, not giving the learner answers. As you prepare, mark those sections that suggest a class activity. Choose the verses that should be looked up in Scripture. What discussion questions will you ask? at what points? Write them in the margin of your study guide. Involve class members, but give them clear directions. What practical actions will you propose for the week following the lesson? A trip to the slums? Interviewing a poor family? Talking about injustice to a county or city administrator? Which of the items do you consider most important for your class?

How will you best use your teaching period? Do you have 45 minutes? an hour? or an hour and a half? If time is short, what should you cut? Learn to become a wise steward of class time.

Be sure to take time to summarize the lesson, or have a class member do it. Plan brief opening and closing devotions using members of the class. Suggestions are provided in the leaders guide. Remember to pray frequently for yourself and your students.

Using Your Resources

The student or teacher cannot get the background—historical, cultural, and theological—for such a book as Hosea by reading only the biblical text. Paragraphs, sentences, phrases, individual words, and expressions can be fully understood only in the light of the times and circumstances in which the prophet lived and spoke. Thus it is important that both student and class leader consult introductory articles in reference works and commentaries. Parishes should provide leaders with some of the essential books by purchasing them for the church library or for the individual teacher's library.

The following are especially recommended:

1. A good, recently revised Bible dictionary or encyclopedia.

2. A good commentary is recommended. The People's Bible Commentary series, available from Concordia Publishing House, is thorough and easily understood.

3. One or more of the recent translations and paraphrases of Hosea: NIV, NRSV, Phillips.

Part 1

Lesson 1
Hosea: God's Messenger (Hosea 1:1–9)

Before the Session

Before the first lesson, read through the book of Hosea. Read through it once quickly to get an overview of the book. Then read through it slowly, using a commentary if possible, to understand it better. You don't need to become an expert on Hosea, but your class will look to you as a resource person, so you should be comfortable with it.

Getting Started

Arrive at your classroom early, especially for this first lesson. Arrange tables and chairs in a comfortable study pattern. Make sure everyone can see the chalkboard or newsprint. Check the thermostat and adjust as necessary. It's hard to concentrate if you are too hot or too cold! Make sure the lighting is adequate enough to read the small print found in many Bibles. Do you have extra Bibles handy? Provide pencils and pens. Encourage the class participants to write notes in their Bibles and to underline key passages.

As participants arrive, encourage conversation among them. Get involved yourself, especially with those whom you do not know well. Just before class time begins, have members introduce themselves.

The Class Session

Open your first class session with this prayer:

> Blessed Lord, who has caused all Holy Scripture, including the book of Hosea, to be written for our learning, grant that we may in such wise hear, read, mark, learn, and inwardly digest Your holy Word, that by patience and comfort of Your Word we may embrace, and ever hold fast, the blessed hope of everlasting life. Amen.

Then read aloud the "Goal" and "What's Going On Here?" Ask for discussion or comments.

Introduce Hosea, the author. Hosea and Amos began their ministry at about the same time, but Hosea's lasted longer (for over 38 years). Hosea was from Israel, the Northern Kingdom (sometimes called Ephraim), and directs his prophecy there. Israel was disintegrating, being torn apart by sin from within and enemies from outside.

Searching the Scriptures

Read aloud or have volunteers read aloud the suggested portions of Scripture before discussing the questions. You may wish to have participants discuss the questions in small groups, if your class is large and if time allows.

The Man and His Mission (Hosea 1:1)

1. Prophets were mere humans, but their teachings came from God. We rejoice that God chooses to use humans as His emissaries, but we are careful not to let anything overshadow God's Word, which brings us the message of the Gospel.

2. The major prophets are Isaiah, Jeremiah, and Ezekiel. The terms *minor prophets* and *major prophets* were adopted because of the sizes of the books, not because of importance. Major or minor, large or small, all these men were inspired by the Holy Spirit to write the words of God.

3. God's word came to Hosea—he was not necessarily looking for it. God told Hosea specifically to marry an unfaithful woman, who would be unfaithful to their marriage vows.

4. The rulers and people of Israel had been unfaithful to God. As a result of this, Israel was being attacked from the outside by other countries and from the inside by their own sinfulness. Hosea's goal was to point out this unfaithfulness so they would realize their sin, repent, and turn back to God before it was too late.

The Man and His Marriage (Hosea 1:2–9)

1. God in wondrous mercy and love made a covenant with the people of Israel even though He knew they were prone to unfaithfulness. And as the book of Hosea goes on to show, when they were unfaithful, the Lord pursued them, seeking to bring them back to Himself in repentance and faith. This same seeking love of God can be seen in the actions of Jesus. Rather than condemning and ostracizing the Samaritan woman and the woman caught in adultery, Jesus sought to bring them back to God.

2. The people of Israel did not acknowledge the Lord as the source of all their material blessings. They also worshiped Baal and the images of golden calves and engaged in fertility worship with the cult prostitutes at the sanctuaries.

3. Hosea was to name his son Jezreel, after the city where Jehu, a former king of Israel, had ordered the slaughter of the 70 sons of the house Ahab **(2 Kings 10:1–11)**. God is not asleep and will not be mocked **(Gal. 6:7)**. God still punishes cruelty and disobedience through civil courts and through the natural outcome of our sinful actions. But God also is merciful and offers forgiveness to those who repent of their sins **(Eph. 2:4–5; Titus 3:5)**.

4. Read **2 Kings 18:13–19:36** for this story of salvation. Sennacherib, the king of Assyria, had threatened Jerusalem and was ready to lay siege to it. Hezekiah, the king of Judah, prayed to the Lord and was assured that God would protect His faithful people. And so He did. He sent His angel to the camp of the Assyrian army to kill the soldiers.

5. *Lo-Ammi* means "not my people." The name of Gomer's third child reflected God's attitude toward His people. Lo-Ammi may not have been Hosea's biological child, but rather the result of Gomer's unfaithfulness. So God was telling the people of Israel that because of their unfaithfulness, they were no longer His people and as such would not benefit from the blessings of the Father.

The Word for Us

1. The Old Testament told about the salvation to come. The New Testament is the fulfillment of that salvation in and through the person and work of Jesus Christ.

2. *Jesus* means "the Lord saves." Answers will vary.

3. Hosea received his call directly from the Lord. It is possible that God put the thought directly into Hosea's mind. God may have also communicated with Hosea through a dream or vision.

4. Discuss the various ways through which God gives us His Word. In the sacraments, Baptism and the Lord's Supper, God's Word of grace comes to us with the natural elements of water, bread, and wine.

5. The chief content of God's Word is the Word made flesh—Jesus Christ—and the salvation He came to bring. See **John 1:1, 14.**

6. Being a Christian does not always mean being popular or doing the easy things. Sometimes it is necessary to distance ourselves from sin and temptation, even if that means leaving our family or a well-paying career. Sometimes it even means suffering physically or emotionally or both.

7. Believers put their trust in their saving God. As sinful humans, it is sometimes difficult to put our trust and faith in someone who can't be seen. But we can see God's record, that He has always been faithful, and we can know with certainty that He will always be faithful in the future.

8. God points out that His love is more powerful than any weapon. Even

more powerful than nuclear weapons! Each name of Hosea's children is more ominous than the last. God uses each name to declare His judgment until finally it is complete. **Ex. 20:5** states God's complete justice and judgment against the permeating affects of sin. Just as sin permeates through the generations, so must judgment. **Ex. 20:6** states that as strong as God's justice is, His love is stronger—not to just three or four generations, but to thousands.

9. Although our sufferings won't earn us a place in heaven, they will often cause us to turn to God for help. Suffering helps us appreciate what Christ went through during His mission on earth and also helps us understand the significance of His mission and what it means for us. When we understand the saving work of Jesus, we can receive it as our own and inherit the kingdom of heaven. Through the person and work of Jesus we receive the forgiveness of sins and eternal life.

Closing

If class members feel comfortable doing so, have them share any suffering and trials they have or are experiencing. Pray for these members, then pray together the stanzas of the hymn.

In anticipation of your next class session, assign opening and closing prayers to participants if they feel comfortable with such a task.

Lesson 2

Reunited or Rebuked? (Hosea 1:10–2:8)

Before the Session

Read through **Hosea 1:10–2:8.** Work through the lesson yourself, jotting down any insights. Are there any unrepentant sins haunting your life? If so, use your study of this lesson to examine yourself and to ask God for His forgiveness.

Getting Started

As class members arrive, give each a piece of paper. Ask the participants to write on the paper any sin that they feel is standing between themselves and God. Then they should place the paper in their Bible but not share it with other class members. If they do not know of any sin that is presently inhibiting their relationship with the Father, they should still put the blank paper in their Bible.

The Class Session

Check to see that everyone has a Bible. Then, if you assigned an opening prayer to a participant, have him or her pray it to begin the class session. Have another class member read aloud the "Goal" and "What's Going On Here?" Encourage the members to comment on these, then read aloud **Hosea 1:10–2:8.** Review Hosea's family and the meaning of their names. In this lesson you will study God's purpose and meaning behind the name of Gomer's third child, Lo-Ammi, and specifically how it relates to the people of Israel.

Searching the Scriptures

The Promise of a Reunion (Hosea 1:10–2:1)

1. In **verse 10,** Hosea says God's people will be too numerous to be counted, just like sand on the seashore. Such growth reflects God's favor to all who believe in Him and walk in His ways.

2. The Israelites will be called "sons of the living God." Unlike idols, which are dead and inanimate, our living God is active in the lives of His people. God speaks to us through His Word, forgives us through His sacraments, comforts us through fellow believers, and listens to us through prayer.

3. The promised reunion is to be understood in a spiritual sense. It began with the Pentecost event **(Acts 2:1–13),** which marked the birthday of the Christian church. The "one leader" is Jesus Christ, the crucified and risen Messiah. The great cruelty once enacted in Jezreel **(Hosea 1:4)** was to yield to "peace to men on whom His favor rests" **(Luke 2:14);** to the saving, sanctifying love of God in Jesus Christ for His New Testament "Israel."

God's Blockade (Hosea 2:2–8)

1. Hosea told his children to rebuke their mother because of her unrepentant sin. Hosea is pointing out that every believer has the responsibility to point out the sinfulness of those around them. In Elijah's day, 7,000 had remained faithful to the Lord.

2. (a) **verse 3**; (b) **verse 4**; (c) **verse 5**; (d) **verse 6**; (e) **verse 7.**

3. God desires more than empty promises; He desires the hearts of His believers.

The Word for Us

1. God's promise to Abraham wasn't just that he would have a lot of descendants. God promised that the Savior of all the nations on earth

would come from Abraham's descendants. Just as God promised salvation to faithful Abraham and Hosea, so He promises salvation to His faithful people today.

2. Jesus warns that a house built on sand will fall **(Matt. 7:26–27)**. If the church builds on anyone or anything other than the true foundation, Jesus Christ **(1 Cor. 3:11),** it too will fall. Encourage your class members to share how God called them into His holy kingdom—through infant Baptism, the witness of family or friends, etc. As members of God's kingdom, we are compelled to witness about the salvation of Jesus to others. Encourage your class members to keep a journal of their witnessing attempts. They should include missed opportunities to make them aware of future opportunities.

3. Although it is true that God looks at souls, not numbers, we are compelled to fulfill the Great Commission to all nations **(Matt. 28:19).** God realized that humans are more apt to think in terms of numbers so He included specific numbers in **Acts 1:15; 2:41;** and **4:4.** See also **Acts 2:47; 5:14; 6:1; 6:7; 7:17; 9:31; 11:21; 11:24; 11:26; 14:1; 14:21; 16:5; 17:4; 17:12; 17:34; 19:26;** and **28:23.**

4. Christians may use every opportunity to testify of their faith, even in the names of their children.

5. Matthew outlines how to confront a sinful brother or sister: First, talk privately with the offender. If he or she doesn't repent, then talk with the offender in the presence of two or three witnesses. If the person is still recalcitrant, make the church aware of the person's unrepentance. If still the person persists in the sin, the church may choose to ban him or her from partaking in Holy Communion. Hopefully, this drastic administration of the Law will awaken the person to his or her sinfulness. When this happens, the person will be receptive to the forgiveness of the Gospel. Pastors, following in the footsteps of the prophet Hosea, especially have the responsibility of rebuking those who fall away. See **2 Sam. 12:1–15; 2 Tim. 4:2;** and **Gal. 6:1.**

6. God promises an abundant life of spiritual blessings. He also notes that life on earth may well contain hardships and sufferings for believers who witness their faith. See **1 Peter 4:12–16.**

7. Although children suffer as a result of their parents' sinful actions, they do not suffer as a punishment for them. For example, if a parent is convicted of stealing and is sent away to prison, the child suffers the results of the crime, namely the loss of parental companionship, but does not receive punishment for the parent's crime. Children today often blame their parents for their behaviors and attitudes. This displaced responsibility can keep a person from confessing his or her sin and receiving the for-

giveness God provides in Jesus Christ.

8. Judas would not believe that God's power to forgive was bigger than his sin and so died unrepentant. Peter, however, understood the full implication of the forgiveness offered by Jesus and willingly received it.

9. God can, also in the lives of Christians today, put thornbushes or obstacles into their path, not as punishment but in order to keep them from trouble or to guide them onto better ways. God put obstacles in Paul's path in order to guide him to where God wanted him to be and to keep his eyes focused on God, not on himself. The outcome of this was that Paul was able to reach more people with the pure Gospel.

10. Whenever God blocks the path of our sinful actions, He opens the door to spiritual blessings, as earned for us by Jesus through His death and resurrection.

Closing

Have the class members remove from their Bibles the sheet of paper on which they wrote any unrepentented sins. Allow them a few moments of silence to confess their sins to their heavenly Father. Then instruct them to tear up the papers (even the blank papers) as you read the following words of Paul:

> Therefore, my brothers [and sisters], I want you to know that through Jesus the forgiveness of sins is proclaimed to you. Through Him everyone who believes is justified from everything you could not be justified from by the law of Moses (**Acts 13:38–39**).

Then have a class member close the session with prayer if someone has volunteered to do so. Or sing or pray together the first stanza of "I Trust, O Christ, in You Alone."

Line up volunteers for the opening and closing prayers for the next class session if you choose.

Lesson 3

The Price of Love (Hosea 2:9–3:5)

Before the Session

Read through **Hosea 2:9–3:5.** How do these verses apply to you? Be prepared to give a witness of how God's love has touched your life. See "The Word for Us," number 5.

Getting Started

Before class time, have any early arrivals write on the chalkboard or newsprint those qualities in a person that make a good spouse. Refer to this list throughout the class session as you talk about the marriage of Hosea to Gomer and that of God to His people.

The Class Session

Have a volunteer from the class open the session with prayer, or do so yourself. Have a class member read aloud the "Goal" and another read "What's Going On Here?"

Review the message of the last session, that God longs to be reunited with His wayward children but will rebuke them if they continue in their sinful ways. Have a class member or members read aloud **Hosea 2:9–3:5.** Then proceed with the lesson.

Searching the Scriptures
Betrayal and Betrothal (Hosea 2:9–23)

1. By withdrawing His earthly blessings (what we refer to in the Lord's Prayer as "our daily bread"), God is hoping to awaken His people to the realization of the source of those blessings, so they turn back to Him for both their earthly and spiritual needs. Israel was in danger of losing its inheritance—its identity as children of the heavenly Father.

2. Other countries saw that, while the people of Israel professed to be the children of the one true God, in practice they worshiped other gods. This fickleness was not lost on other nations, especially Assyria, who used it to its advantage to get a foothold in the country and then seized it and deported the people.

3. God is a jealous God, demanding the undivided devotion of His people. (See **Ex. 20:5.**) God knows that humans cannot be fully dedicated to more than one thing.

4. God promised grace and peace, joy and hope, to a penitent and believing people. He sought to be like a loving, forgiving husband who would not give up on his wayward wife. Compare these qualities to the list you made before class. **Verses 19–20** sparkle like Gospel gems. They are a declaration of God's abiding love and compassion through Christ, the Mediator.

5. Jesus says that He gives His people eternal life and protects them from those who seek to lure them away. God takes the cursed names of His children and turns them, 180 degrees, into blessings by His grace, giving His everlasting identity to His children. God's people respond by affirming their relationship with their heavenly Father.

Love to the Unloving (Hosea 3)

1. Hosea is to smother his adulterous wife with love and forgiveness to show Israel how their God has done the same to them. Just as Gomer had turned to other lovers to receive gifts and attention, so Israel had turned to other countries and idols to receive benefits and power. The result of this turning to others is best described by the words *destitute* and *powerless*.

2. The price God paid to buy us back from the slavery of our sin was much greater than a few shekels of silver. He paid with the life of His only Son, Jesus.

3. To marry and live with a known prostitute was unthinkable in Hosea's time—yet he did so to show Gomer how much he loved her. All Hosea asked in return was Gomer's faithfulness. Likewise, our Lord suffered humiliation to come to earth to die to redeem us from our sins. All He asks in return is our faithfulness. Ask, Did you write *love* and *faithfulness* on the list you made before class?

4. In **Hosea 3:5,** as in many places in Scripture, the Messiah is referred to as David. Peter makes it clear in his sermon that although David was a mighty king on this earth, his descendant Jesus was the holy King of all of heaven and earth.

The Word for Us

1. God, like a bridegroom, gives Himself fully to His bride, the church—so much so that He was willing to die for her. Ask, "Was this trait mentioned on the list you made before class?" We (the church) respond as a bride who is willing to follow faithfully the groom's lead, because she knows that the groom will always provide for her needs and will protect her from all harm.

2. Paul makes it clear that when attempts are made to meld false teachings with the teachings of Christ, the result is not a harmonious blend, but rather a vile corruption of God's holy Word. The Gospel is lost and false superstitions take its place.

3. The "door of hope" is God's open invitation to repentance. Our only hope can come from God our Savior.

Your Bible study group may want to reach out to a charity to support not just with money or goods but by sharing the Gospel message with those scattered by misfortune.

4. God is active in every aspect of a believer's life. In nature, God responds to our needs for sunshine, water, air, etc. These gifts have been corrupted by sin's invasion into the world, however. Thus we have drought and floods, earthquakes, hurricanes, and other natural disasters. In history, God is not a puppeteer who manipulates events and people, but rather He

makes Himself known through the events of history, showing His grace when humans set out to harm one another. Occasionally, people will listen to their conscience and hear God's Law. When they do so, they are then open to receive His holy Gospel. Often people do not listen to their conscience; therefore God wrote down His Law in the form of the Ten Commandments. To a world enslaved by sin, God responds with His Gospel, the message of salvation through His Son Jesus Christ.

5. Share with the class how God has shown His love and saving grace in your life. As time permits, encourage class members to do likewise.

6. Marriage is the closest earthly bond between two people. It is based on trust, faithfulness, and commitment. When one partner breaks this bond, it leaves the other vulnerable and hurt. In addition, husbands are to love their wives and be considerate, respectful, and protective of them. Surprisingly, God never commands that wives must love their husbands. God knows that if love and respect are given by a husband, his wife will usually respond with love and respect. The Bible uses the word *submissive* to describe this response of a wife for her husband. A husband should not expect his wife to be submissive; he must earn that honor. Compare the qualities discussed here to the list you made before class.

7. The price God paid to buy us back from slavery was the life of His Son, Jesus. God made the supreme sacrifice for us. We respond with love and faithfulness to Him.

Closing

Sing or pray together the words of the hymn "Chief of Sinners Though I Be." Then have a volunteer close with prayer, or do so yourself. Ask for volunteers to lead the opening prayer in the next session.

Part 2

Lesson 4
An Unfaithful People (Hosea 4:1–5:7)

Before the Session
In preparation for this lesson, gather newspaper clippings dealing with sins and crimes corresponding to those mentioned in **Hosea 4:2:** "cursing, lying and murder, stealing and adultery ... bloodshed follows bloodshed."

Getting Started
Display the clippings you gathered. Tell the participants to match the clippings with Paul's list of sinful acts in **Gal. 5:19–21.** What, beyond crime bills, gun control, and more laws, is needed to effect a change? Draw from **Gal. 5:22–26.**

The Class Session
Have a volunteer from the class open the session with prayer, or do so yourself. Have a class member read aloud the "Goal" and another read "What's Going On Here?" Discuss each briefly.

Searching the Scriptures
Sin Creates Shortages (Hosea 4)
Read aloud **Hosea 4.**

1. The Israelites are missing faithfulness to, love for, and acknowledgement of the one true God. Jesus makes it clear that the most important thing is to love God.

2. Compare the sins and outcomes in **Hosea 4:2–3** to those listed in your newspaper clippings.

3. The priests and prophets were not teaching the people God's Word, but rather leading them in the worship of false gods. As a result of this, the people were going to lose their mother (i.e., their land) and their own identity.

4. God has made a covenant, like a marriage agreement, with His people. When they are unfaithful to God, they break the covenant and in effect commit spiritual adultery. Part of the worship of Baal included cult prostitution **(4:14).**

5. It may be that the Israelites learned to worship calves in Egypt, where Apis, the sacred bull, was venerated. Or they may have picked up the custom from the Canaanites and Phoenicians, who worshiped Baal, who was believed to give fertility to the womb and life-giving rain to the soil. Baal was pictured as standing on a bull, a symbol of strength and fertility, with a storm cloud as his chariot, thunder as his voice, and lightning as his spear and arrows. Sacred prostitution and sometimes child sacrifice were part of Baal worship.

God's Red Alert (Hosea 5:1–7)

1. The royal house had set traps, as it were, to induce the people to worship idols set up in the places mentioned (here, Mizpah and Tabor; elsewhere, Gilgal and Beth Aven), to keep the people from worshiping in Jerusalem. The priests had gone along with these mistruths. Those guilty of idolatry—from the king to the priests to the people—would be killed or taken from their land.

2. The people were deep into idolatry and corruption. They desired to be a powerful nation and would do anything to become so—even to the point of selling out God, and ultimately as a result of this, their souls. They arrogantly denied the sovereignty of the Lord. They thought of themselves as all-powerful, but the king of Assyria soon showed them how wrong they were. To approach God, the people must confess their sinful behavior, admit that they are powerless against sin, and ask God for forgiveness and help.

3. The sins of Israel would be copied by Judah, and in time that nation too would fall.

The Word for Us

1. God entrusted the care of the world to us **(Gen. 1:28–30),** so we want to live up to His trust. Stewardship of the earth includes caring for God's creation in the best way to spread the Gospel. We should share with others our reason for caring for God's creation and use every opportunity to share the Gospel.

2. Pastors are human beings and as such are tempted. This does not excuse their sinful actions, however. More than anyone, pastors should know the importance of filling their minds and hearts with the Gospel, blocking out sinful thoughts and usurping sinful actions **(Col. 3:2).** It is no accident that Jesus tells us to "love the Lord your God with all your heart and with all your soul and with all your *mind*" (**Matt. 22:37;** emphasis added).

3. Have class members share the forms of idolatry offered by other cults and religions, advertising, greed, etc. Write each idol on the chalkboard or

newsprint, then draw a cross through each to show that Jesus is more powerful than any idol. Read aloud **Rom. 1:16** and **Phil. 3:10**.

4. **Leviticus 4–8** lists the guidelines for animal sacrifice in the Old Testament. The type of animal to be sacrificed depended on the purpose of the sacrifice. (See p. 150 of the Concordia Self-Study Bible for a table of Old Testament sacrifices.) The blood was to signify the washing away of the people's sins. When Jesus shed His blood on the cross, He washed away the sins of the whole world, once for all time.

5. It is good to acknowledge God's hand in creation, but we must always remember that God is a jealous God **(Ex. 20:5)** and demands that we worship only Him. If you have time, you may want to discuss the New Age Movement, which emphasizes the cycles of nature and the power of the sun, moon, and stars. Good resources for this are *The New Age Is Lying to You*, by Eldon K. Winker (CPH, 1994) and *The New Age Movement* in the How to Respond series, by Philip H. Lochhaas (CPH, 1988, 1995).

6. As the participants discuss this question, guide the discussion to keep it from becoming a gripe contest. Remind the participants that we are to be loving examples of the Gospel to the people of this world.

7. Christians regard material possessions as gifts from God, the Creator of all matter, and use such possessions as best as possible to the glory of God and to spread the Gospel. Material objects come and go; only God is unchanging. He is the only one who can meet all of our needs.

8. Guide the participants in their discussion to realize that God never leaves His people crushed by the Law; He always provides the promise of the Gospel.

Closing

Give the participants a few minutes to silently meditate on **Hosea 4:1–5:7** and confess any sins about which they feel guilt. Then lead them in singing or saying the stanzas of "Jesus Sinners Will Receive." Conclude with this declaration of grace: Your sins are washed away by the blood of Jesus. You are forgiven. Go in peace and serve the Lord.

Lesson 5
The Sacrifice of Mercy (Hosea 5:8–6:10)

Before the Session

Read through **Hosea 5:8–6:10.** Study these verses in a commentary if one is available. Pray for your class participants, that the Holy Spirit would help them understand this passage.

If possible, display a map of Israel and Judah, such as that on page 494 of the Concordia Self-Study Bible. Mark on the map the location of Ephraim (Israel), Judah, Gibeah, Ramah, and Beth Aven (Bethel).

Getting Started

As participants arrive, encourage them to examine the map you have on display. If you do not have a map on display, have them examine together the maps in the back of their Bibles. Don't feel that you have to teach a geography lesson; just let them explore to find the places mentioned in **Hosea 5:8–15.**

If a map is unavailable, have members skim through **1 Kings 12:1–30** and discuss how the 10 northern tribes seceded from the union of the 12 tribes formed by King David. Ask the members to find the political, geographical, and spiritual motives for the division.

The Class Session

Begin with prayer, lead by a class participant, if possible. Ask a class member to read the "Goal" and another to read "What's Going On Here?" Ask for questions and comments. Then point out Israel and Judah on the map. Remind participants that the Northern Kingdom, Israel, was also called Ephraim, after one of the 10 tribes. Ephraim was Joseph's son. The tribe of Benjamin, together with Judah, constituted the Southern Kingdom with Jerusalem as headquarters.

Searching the Scriptures
The Plague on Both Houses (Hosea 5:8–15)

Read or have a participant read **Hosea 5:8–15.** On the chalkboard or newsprint, write all the "like" parables from this selection ("like those who move boundary stones"; "like a flood of water"; "like a moth"; "like rot"; "like a lion"). These will be discussed during the lesson.

1. Hosea states with certainty that Ephraim (Israel) will be totally destroyed—and indeed it was. Judah would later follow suit. God's people

had put their faith in an earthly kingdom, rather than in the heavenly King who had provided them with a homeland. After their land was destroyed, the people had nowhere to turn but to God, who promised to rebuild Israel not as an earthly kingdom but as the kingdom of all believers. See **Rom. 11:25–27.**

2. In **Deut. 19:14; Job 24:2;** and **Prov. 23:10** God commands that landmarks not be changed. Such an act can lead to war and distrust among nations. Judah, like Israel, was losing sight of the boundary between right and wrong and would find itself, like Israel, utterly destroyed.

3. Instead of placing its faith in the heavenly Father, Israel made an alliance or covenant with Assyria. Then, to make matters worse, Israel angered Assyria by not keeping the covenant. It did not pay the required tribute, and it conspired with another country. Hosea warned Israel of the consequences of this—total destruction.

4. In His omniscience, God waits until all hope for repentance is gone.

5. God's wrath is like a flood that utterly washes away everything in its path, leaving nothing recognizable behind.

A Standing Invitation (Hosea 6:1–10)

1. The people were sinful, and God must punish sin. Jesus, the Messiah, took on Himself the sins of all the world. Those who believe this promise receive it, even if they believed it before it was fulfilled.

2. Hosea offered to his wife salvation from her wicked ways **(chap. 3).** Hosea records God's offer of salvation to Israel and Judah **(2:14–23; 6:1–2).**

3. **Hosea 6:2** tells that God revives us to life and may hint that this is through the death and resurrection of Jesus, who was three days in the grave.

4. Knowing Christ is so exciting that we want to tell the whole world. Even though our sinful nature often gets in the way, God's Spirit is stronger, and we live to please the Lord. This does not go unnoticed by others.

5. Ephraim and Judah repented only when it was convenient for them, and then insincerely and for only a short while. God does not accept lukewarm repentance **(Rev. 3:16)** but demands complete devotion. Because they were not sincere, God destroyed their land and scattered them throughout the world.

6. We worship God "in spirit and in truth" when we worship Him—and only Him—with our whole heart and in every aspect of our lives, including our dealings with other people. By showing kindness and love to others (our neighbors), we are showing kindness and love to God.

The Word for Us

1. Many physical and emotional ailments are manifestations of spiritual ailments. When one is at peace with God, then peace of mind will follow, and oftentimes physical healing as well. Jesus often explained this association of spiritual and physical healing—but was not fully understood by His followers, who continued to ask for physical healing only. See **Matt. 8:5–13; 9:1–8; 9:20–22; 9:27–31; 15:21–28; Mark 9:14–29; John 5:14.**

2. At times a parent has to turn away from an errant child to restrain himself or herself from harming the child in anger. God also turns away from His sinful children for He abhors their wickedness. Just as the parent then turns back to the child because love is greater than anger, so God turns back to His children with love and forgiveness. The saying goes that God only moves away as far as we move from Him. If we are willing to receive God's comfort, He provides it.

3. Misery is a result of our sinfulness. Only God can give true relief from the misery of sin. God works miracles every day by turning our sinful, inward-looking hearts into joyful hearts that can see the good that God has done.

4. The Law shows us our sins; the Gospel shows us God's salvation. Hosea made it clear that Israel and Judah's sinful actions were not pleasing to God, but He would forgive and sustain them if they repented. They did not repent and therefore Hosea had to return to the Law. Even today there are people who will not take God's Law seriously and therefore will not be able to understand the Gospel. When we preach only the Gospel to these people they get the idea that God is a "sugar daddy" in heaven who automatically grants eternal life to everyone. This false teaching is called "universalism." Thus Jesus' death and resurrection are reduced to nothing. Just as in Hosea's day, the Gospel is ineffective without the Law.

5. Hosea repeatedly points out the people's sins and what will be the result of these. Time and again he also offers them a chance to repent and turn back to God. Other Scripture writers repeat this pattern, from Moses **(Genesis)** to John **(Revelation).** Although we New Testament believers have the advantage of knowing our Savior by name, Old Testament believers knew the promise that God was sending a Messiah (Savior).

6. In sin, people sometimes assume that the more they give, the more they will find favor in God's eyes. What they forget is that God only desired one sacrifice—that of Jesus Christ. Now He desires that we believe in Jesus and share His love with others.

7. Our sinful nature, which was drowned by Baptism, tries to resurface every day. Martin Luther wrote that it is important for Christians to renew their baptismal vows every day to keep their old sinful nature (sometimes called the Old Adam) in check: "[Baptizing with water] indicates that the

Old Adam in us should by daily contrition and repentance be drowned and die with all sins and evil desires, and that a new man should daily emerge and arise to live before God in righteousness and purity forever" (Luther's Small Catechism).

8. Although individual faith is important, God made humans to be social creatures. We are to use the corporate structure of the church to support and build up one another in the faith.

Closing

Sing or speak the stanzas of "In Adam We Have All Been One" as a prayer. Encourage the class members to greet one another outside of class with "The Lord be with you," and then to respond with "And also with you." Have a class member close the session with prayer if someone has volunteered to do so.

Lesson 6
Longing for Repentance (Hosea 6:11–8:14)

Before the Session

Read through **Hosea 6:11–8:14** to prepare for class. Have several Bible concordances available for the members to use as they arrive for class.

Getting Started

"I long to redeem them," the Lord declares through Hosea **(7:13)**. As class members arrive, have them use a Bible concordance to write their own summary of what God's universal grace entails. Have them look for words like *redeem, Redeemer, save, Savior, whole world.* Wrap up the activity and prepare for the class session by reading **1 John 2:2**.

The Class Session

Have a volunteer begin the class session with prayer if one has agreed to do so. Have a class member read aloud the "Goal" section of the study guide and another read "What's Going On Here?" Ask for questions and comments.

Searching the Scriptures

God's Yes, People's No (Hosea 6:11–7:16)

1. There is no sin committed that God does not see. Times may change but sin remains the same throughout generations. Even governments are corrupt and sinful. In Israel, King Elah had been killed during a drunken celebration and his throne taken by his assassin **(1 Kings 16:8–10).** Generally, the faithfulness of the king was reflected by the faithfulness of the people. National and religious holidays became nothing more than occasions for sin and drunkenness.

2. Israel foolishly tried to make alliances with both Egypt and Assyria. This would lead to its political downfall when Assyria demanded—and took—full control of Israel. Doves are timid birds who try to act tough but don't often succeed in fooling their enemies. Israel likewise tried to act tough in its alliances but didn't realize that all the while Assyria was stalking it for the kill. People, like doves, often think that they are strong enough or tough enough to handle any situation themselves—but are actually weak and sinful and thus easily overrun. Full protection only comes in the power of the Lord Almighty.

3. God says He will throw a net around His people and pull them down. Birds caught in a net become entangled and cannot escape. There is no escaping God's judgment. Here are some other references in Scripture to the use of nets in hunting and fishing: **Hab. 1:15; Ps. 35:7–8; Matt. 4:18.**

4. God says that He longs to heal and redeem (buy back) His people. Scripture consists of God's plan of grace for the sinful world.

5. Whenever we try to solve our own problems we end up deeper and deeper in trouble. If we repent and seek the Lord through His Word, He will direct us and lead us out of our sinful behavior.

Tarnish on the Golden Calf (Hosea 8)

1. God is not mocked or deceived **(Gal. 6:7).** He saw through the Israelites' pretenses into their unrepentant hearts.

2. The people were to throw out their idols and break them to pieces before they themselves were thrown out of their country and scattered like broken pieces throughout other lands.

3. In addition to idolatry, the Israelites had broken every other commandment. Adultery was commonplace. They coveted after the wealth of other nations. They lied to their political allies, etc. Hosea compared Israel to a healthy-looking crop that produced no grain.

4. Israel had been a unique nation, chosen by God. But when it allied itself with Assyria and Egypt, it conformed to the other nations and gave up its identity and its God. Now it was like a wild donkey wandering alone

without a master.

5. In an attempt to appease God, the people went through the motions of sacrifice—but their hearts and faith were not in it. Sacrifice without faith is an abomination to the Lord and leads to damnation rather than salvation.

The Word for Us

1. God is omniscient—He knows everything about us. This means you can't "get away" with any sinful behavior—He sees it all. More importantly, though, this means that God is always there when you need Him. The prayer lines are always open. God is always ready to dispense His forgiveness, which leads to peace.

2. Moral breakdown leads to societal breakdown. Sin reigns. The only answer to sin is Jesus. Out of thanks for Jesus' saving actions, Christians strive to live as Jesus did **(1 Cor. 1:11; Titus 2:7)**, showing the love and compassion that our Savior showed, so that others will turn from their sinful ways and seek His pure way. This Christian lifestyle begins with training at home **(Prov. 22:6)**. If there is time, have class members explain and apply this saying: "The heart of Christian education is the education of the heart."

3. Discuss what goes on at Christmas office parties, New Year's Eve celebrations, Mardi Gras carnivals before Lent. *Mardi Gras* literally means "Fat Tuesday"; *carnival* is from the Latin *caro* and *levare:* good-bye meat. Paul exhorts us to be sober and decent at all times. We should always ask ourselves if our behavior is pleasing to God and if it is a reflection of Christ.

4. James warns believers to listen more, talk less, and avoid unrighteous anger. Longing becomes theft; envy and/or hatred becomes murder; lust becomes adultery; jealousy becomes slander—the list goes on and on. See **Matt. 15:19; 1 Cor. 6:9–10; Gal. 5:19; Eph. 5:3–4;** and **James 1:15.**

5. God promised the people of Israel their own land, their own God, freedom, plenty of food, housing, and an identity. Their only responsibility was to be God's people—have faith in God alone and obey His commandments. From the outset, the people of Israel broke the commandments and worshiped false gods and idols. In Baptism, God blesses His children with faith, forgiveness of sins, and salvation. God gives us faith in Baptism. Working through God's Word the Holy Spirit empowers us to remain faithful.

6. Discuss the many idols that people worship today. With so many outside pressures, people need help to resist temptation. The Holy Spirit strengthens and preserves our faith through God's Word to live lives that reflect God's love for us.

7. Like the Israelites, people today choose to keep sinning rather than to receive the freedom of Christ's forgiveness. Unrepented sin begins a spiral effect of more sin and unhappiness and frustration with life. Only repentance and forgiveness by Jesus can rescue us from the bondage of sin.

8. There is nothing we can do to earn God's forgiveness and salvation. All we can do is praise God for being who He is—a loving, merciful God. God listens to our praise with joyfulness as a parent listens to a child's acclamation of love.

Closing

Sing or pray together the hymn stanzas. If you have assigned a closing prayer to a class member, have that person close with prayer. Otherwise do so yourself, praising God for His greatness and asking Him for forgiveness and also for guidance to live as His children.

Lesson 7

Adding Up the Sinfulness (Hosea 9–10)

Before the Session

If possible, have available a map of the ancient Middle East with Israel, Memphis, Gibeah, Mount Peor (or Baal Peor, near Mount Nebo), and Gilgal marked.

Getting Started

The 10 tribes, carried away into captivity by the Assyrians, never returned. They were absorbed—"swallowed up" **(Hosea 8:7–8)** by foreigners. Have participants read **2 Kings 17** and then list on the chalkboard or newsprint what happened at the beginning of Israel's exile. Ask, "By whom was the land resettled?"

The colonists, called "Samaritans," bitterly opposed the return of the Jews and the rebuilding of Jerusalem, its walls, and its temple **(Neh. 4:1–3)**. Some became converts to Christianity **(John 4:39)**, thanks to Jesus' presence among them.

The Class Session

Have a class member lead an opening prayer. Have another volunteer read the "Goal" and "What's Going On Here?" sections. If you have a map available, locate the places mentioned in "What's Going On Here?"

Searching the Scriptures
Time to Pay the Piper (Hosea 9)

1. The Israelites would not be able to worship God in the temple, nor offer sacrifices to Him. Their worship would take on the form of that of the people in the foreign land where they lived.

2. God expects His watchmen (our spiritual leaders) to be upright and trustworthy. We are to obey the watchmen and pray for them.

3. By worshiping Baal and other idols, the Israelites had broken their covenant relationship with God and were no longer worthy of His promises.

4. Sin begins with a thought, a temptation. See **Gen. 3:1–3.** Temptation leads to desire. See **Gen. 3:4–5.** Desire leads to sin. See **Gen. 3:6.** Sin leads to death. See **Gen. 3:19.**

5. Evil taking its course:

Must leave the land **(v. 3).**
Will be made slaves **(v. 6).**
Babies and children will die **(vv. 14, 16).**
Will have bad and rebellious leaders **(v. 15).**
Won't be able to raise food **(v. 16).**
Will be rejected by God **(v. 17).**
Good withheld:
Lack of food and drink **(v. 2).**
Won't be able to worship the Lord **(v. 4).**
Will lose their wealth **(v. 6).**
Will lose their spiritual leaders **(v. 8).**
Will lose population and prosperity **(v. 11).**
Their children will not know God **(v. 12).**
Won't have God's love **(v. 15).**

6. Here are some verses where God proclaimed His love for the Israelites: **2:1, 14–23; 3:1; 7:13.**

Sowing and Reaping with God's Blessing (Hosea 10)

1. At first the people prospered and were thankful to God for their prosperity and land. Then they began to forget who was providing for them and began to worship Baal and other idols. Their jealous God, however, would not tolerate this and would destroy their false altars.

2. The people were pessimistic about future kings and leaders because of the actions of past kings, many of whom were distrustful and harmful. Because of its unfaithfulness to God, Israel was invaded and conquered by Assyria. Its people were scattered into other lands and their nation obliter-

ated. Shalman (perhaps the same as Shalmaneser) of Assyria apparently had already begun the conquest of the Northern Kingdom by the destruction of the fortress city of Beth Arbel with the terrible atrocities described in **10:14.** The conquest was completed in 722 B.C.

3. The fruit of God's unfailing love is salvation and forgiveness in Christ, whose righteousness clothes believers. Then comes the fruit of the Spirit **(Gal. 5:22–25).**

The Word for Us

1. The only thing sin earns is death.

2. Christ gives each of us peace of heart, which is shown in our relationships with others, especially our family.

3. Our response to Christ's forgiveness is to live for Him and to live like Him, full of love, compassion, and kindness. We want to obey God's Law, and by so doing, society is a better place. **Proverbs 14** points out that God's people build up one another, are upright in their dealings, clean in their speech, hardworking, and truthful. They seek God's wisdom, avoid evil situations and people, are prudent in their dealings, and give to others. They are joyful, full of fear and respect of the Lord, patient, kind. They plan to do only what is good. **Rom. 13:1–7** adds that God's people obey the authorities and do what is right.

4. Our response to the Gospel is to desire to live for and like Christ. The Holy Spirit working through God's Word empowers us to do so.

5. Jesus accurately foretold how Jerusalem would be captured and destroyed. As our fortress, Jesus takes on Himself God's judgment for our sins and serves as our stronghold and refuge when we are spiritually vulnerable.

6. As long as there is sin in the world, people will wage war and kill one another. War is never of itself just, but at times involvement in war is justified. **Rom. 13:1–5** describes our Christian responsibility to our temporal government. Included in this responsibility is the prerogative to defend one's country and fellow human beings. You may want to read what the Augsburg Confession says in Article XVI about engaging in "just wars." For more information about just wars, see the CPH Bible study *War: The Christian Response*, by Donald W. Sandmann (1991).

7. Jesus pointed out the miracle that where a little love and kindness is sown, much will be harvested. In **Gal. 6:8,** Paul speaks of sowing to the Spirit and from Him receiving eternal life, not as something earned but as a free gift of grace.

Closing

Have a volunteer (or volunteers) read **Psalm 46.** Then pray together or sing the stanzas to "A Mighty Fortress Is Our God." Close with a prayer led by a volunteer. Or offer a prayer praising God for His judgment and strength and proclaiming our need of Him and His salvation.

Part 3

Lesson 8

True Prophets vs. False Profits
(Hosea 11–12)

Before the Session

Reevaluate your class setting. Do you have enough Bibles? Is the room temperate? Is the seating adequate and comfortable?

Reevaluate your class members. Do they respond to the questions asked in the study? Is there active give-and-take discussion among them? Is there discussion that indicates that the lessons learned in class are being lived out through the week?

Getting Started

As the participants gather for class, have them compare **Hosea 11:1** with **Matt. 2:15** to note the parallelism of God calling both His beloved Israel and His beloved Son out of Egypt. Encourage participants to explain why Matthew was quite proper to apply the Hosea text to Jesus. Jesus came to be the perfectly obedient Son that Israel never was. He retraced steps in Israel's history (see "The Word for Us," number 2).

The Class Session

Have a volunteer open the session with prayer. Then have another class member read the "Goal" and "What's Going On Here?" sections. Ask for questions or comments.

Searching the Scriptures

God's Love: The Tie That Binds (Hosea 11:1–11)

1. In God's eyes, Israel was always His child—and we are His children. Just as He called the nation of Israel His son, so He calls us sons and daughters (**2 Cor. 6:18**). Along with His commandments, God gave Israel a free will. If Israel had used that will to live as God's child, it would have avoided discipline. However, it rebelled against its loving Father and followed a sinful life instead.

2. God disciplined Israel through exile imposed by Assyria. In this way, Israel returned to a slavery similar to that which God rescued it from in Egypt. God stated that "even if they call to the Most High, He will by no means exalt them" (**11:7**).

3. God's love and patience are perfect; He shows love to even the most wicked sinners, unlike humans who are not capable of such a thing. God keeps offering His forgiveness to sinners, and even though He must punish their sins, He withholds His total destruction. We limit God's compassion when we don't receive His forgiveness. Note: Admah and Zeboiim were wicked cities destroyed with Sodom and Gomorrah.

4. Hosea tells how God's people will return to their land repentant and trembling with fear of the Lord.

Prosperous but Perverse (Hosea 11:12–12:14)

1. Hosea recounts the events of Jacob wrestling with God (**Gen. 32:22–32**) and building an altar at Bethel (**Gen. 35:1–5**). Throughout his life, Jacob continually returned to God in repentance and then responded to God's forgiveness with love and justice.

2. Just as the merchants were using weighted and inaccurate scales to measure their goods, so the people were using dishonest standards to delude themselves into thinking they were not sinful. They believed that if they appeared prosperous and wholesome on the outside, others would not see the sinfulness and emptiness on the inside.

3. In the past, God had released His children from slavery and provided a home for them. Now, unless they repented, He would take away their home and allow them to be slaves again. God had always communicated to His people through prophets. The writings of some of God's prophets are compiled in the Holy Bible. Note: Gilead and Gilgal (both corrupt) represent the eastern and western parts of Ephraim.

4. Moses was not just a caravan leader; he was God's spokesman and recorder. The greatest prophet was Jesus, God Himself. Jesus was not only a prophet: He was the fulfillment of prophecy. The Israelites reacted to

God's care with contempt and disrespect. Note: Aram, where Jacob lived with Laban, is Syria.

The Word for Us

1. It is not God who changed; it is our view of God that changed. God always communicates with us in terms we can understand. He condescends to our level. *Anthropopathism* means that God expresses His thoughts and emotions as a human being would.

2. Several scenes from Jesus' life reflect the life of the people of Israel. Jesus' obedience and reliance on God in the desert was the antithesis of the Israelites' testing God, grumbling, and idolatry. In addition, Jesus was baptized in the Jordan River—the same river the Israelites crossed to enter the Promised Land. Jesus, as an infant, fled to Egypt for safety. The infant nation of Israel fled to Egypt during the time of Joseph to escape famine. Jesus walked on water. The Israelites walked through the Red Sea. Encourage your class members to find more examples.

3. God's love would be powerless without His righteousness. His righteousness would be meaningless without His love. We need one to appreciate the other.

4. God can judge people's hearts; He knows when their faith is sincere. Some people, like Saul, demand that God answer them in the way they want Him to and refuse to listen to His Word. Isaiah and Jesus both felt God's abandonment because of the sins they were surrounded by or were carrying. Christ has paid for our sins on the cross, so now when God looks at us, He sees us redeemed through Jesus.

5. People who postpone repentance are postponing the chance for a full life with Christ—our eternal life begins on earth, not just when we reach heaven **(John 17:3; 1 Tim. 6:12; 1 John 5:13)**. Postponing repentance also promotes additional folly for it assumes that people can repent of their own power at a time they may choose. Only the Holy Spirit working through God's Word can bring a person to repentance. On their own, people would never choose to repent. Postponing repentance is rejecting God's grace.

6. Allow the participants to discuss their experiences with other religions. Exercise caution to prevent this from becoming a gripe fest. Rather draw the group into the realization that Jesus is the only bread of life whereby we can be filled to satisfaction **(John 6:35)**.

7. The verses cited refer to the need for people to repent, act in justice and love, and patiently look to the Lord for guidance and hope.

8. Acts sown in love reap love. Christ is the fulfillment of love: He gave Himself for our salvation. Empowered by the Holy Spirit, we respond by giving ourselves to Him.

9. Jesus was the fulfillment of all prophecy, so any revelation claimed by modern-day prophets must be weighed against what He said and what His spokesmen (the prophets) have said and have written in Scripture.

Closing

Sing or pray together the stanzas of "Thy Strong Word." Then close in prayer, led by a volunteer if possible.

Lesson 9

The King's Edict (Hosea 13)

Before the Session

If possible, take photographs of various religious images, figures, and symbols found in your church building (e.g., crosses, stained-glass windows, murals or paintings, statues). Bring these photos to class for the opening discussion. Or bring a few smaller religious objects to class (e.g., small cross, altar or pulpit paraments, candelabra).

Getting Started

As class members arrive, show the photographs or display the objects that symbolize aspects of our Christian faith. Point out that in **chapter 13,** Hosea makes reference to "cleverly fashioned images, all of them the work of craftsmen" **(v. 2).** Solomon's temple also contained cherubs and other figures. See **1 Kings 6.** Discuss the meaning behind each church image. Have class members divide the objects or photos into those images that are used for atmosphere (edification) and those used for adoration. It should come out that although these images are helpful for our worship, it is only God that we adore.

The Class Session

Have a class member open the session with prayer, or sing "Father, I Adore You":

> Father, I adore You,
> Lay my life before You.
> How I love You;

Jesus, I adore You,
Lay my life before You.
How I love You;

Spirit, I adore You,
Lay my life before You.
How I love You;

Then ask a class member to read aloud the "Goal" and "What's Going On Here?" sections. Ask for any questions or comments before beginning the lesson.

Searching the Scriptures

One God, One Savior, One People (Hosea 13:1–8)

1. As Ephraim grew as a country, it embraced the customs and religious practices of the other cultures with which it came into contact. Fertility worship, or the worship of Baal, was strong throughout all of the Middle East and was usually symbolized by a warrior (Baal) on a bull (calf) or just a bull. The Israelites went about incorporating these images into their worship of God, perhaps trying to give a form to their object of devotion. What they forgot, of course, is that God is too great to be confined to an earthly object and that He had specifically warned His people, "You shall not make for yourself an idol in the form of anything in heaven above or on the earth beneath or in the waters below" **(Ex. 20:4).** God knew that humans have a difficult time separating the object from the devotion and would eventually forsake Him altogether in favor of the object. And so it happened. The people began to kiss the graven images to show absolute homage and to offer human sacrifice to Baal. Hosea points out that this worship is shallow and empty, with about as much substance as mist or dew or chaff or smoke.

2. The cult surrounding a man-made idol demands that humans serve the idol and protect it. The true God serves His people and protects them. Being temporal, a man-made idol offers no hope for life after death, unlike our heavenly Father who sacrificed His only Son so His children might live forever. God is the God of and for His people. He desires a personal relationship with each of His children, as He outlined in His covenant with them through Moses and again through Jesus. God continually provided for the Israelites with food, home, protection, and salvation. He does the same for His children today. The Israelites forgot the source of all these gifts and began to be proud of themselves. This unbelief would lead to

God's wrath and destruction.

3. The Old Testament contains many of these prophecies, beginning with **Gen. 3:15.** A few others include **Gen. 49:10; Deut. 18:15; 2 Sam. 7:16; Psalm 110; Isaiah 19:20; 35:4–6; 42:1–4; 53; 62:11;** and **Jer. 33:22.**

4. God has gathered His people together in one true faith: that people are sinful and need a Savior and that the only Savior who can atone for that sin is Jesus Christ. Those who believe this God calls His children (or church).

From Death to Life (Hosea 13:9–16)

1. The Lord, who had given Israel a king, now took away not only their king, but also their kingdom.

2. The Lord has recorded the sins of Israel. Like a mother, the Lord had created, nurtured, and protected the children of Israel. Sin is folly; those who live in it bring about their doom **(Prov. 5:22–23).** A sense of humor is implied in the second part of **Hosea 13:13,** as if to say: "Israel, you didn't have enough sense to know when it was time for you to be born."

3. Read aloud as a class **Hosea 13:14.** Then read aloud **1 Cor. 15:55–57.** Encourage class members to share the feelings these verses elicit in them.

4. This is not a contradiction, not an indication of a change in God's saving purpose. Even though He has continually offered the Israelites His mercy, they have refused to repent. Therefore they must feel the punishment for their sins: "It is a dreadful thing to fall into the hands of the living God" **(Heb. 10:31).** The dry east wind refers to Assyria, which would come and wipe out the fruitful land of Ephraim and commit horrible atrocities. God will show no compassion, which would allow the sinfulness to live on. Likewise He would show no compassion on Jesus but require Him to die for our sinfulness.

The Word for Us

1. People then, as now, put their trust in earthly rulers, family, self, material goods, physical pleasures, etc.

2. People today are sacrificed through human exploitation, especially of children; street murders; the abortion of the unborn. On the latter point, consider the difference between child sacrifices to please a god (like Molech in **Lev. 18:21**) and to please human beings. Like the Israelites, we are often guilty of creating and worshiping the god of self.

3. "Kiss the Son" **(Ps. 2:12)** is what Christians do in their devotion to Jesus Christ, their Savior. Obviously we are not to kiss a statue or icon of

Jesus but to worship Him only as our Lord and Savior and obey His teachings, showing love and mercy to others.

4. God gives us all we need for our life on earth (food, clothing, family) and all we need for our life after earth (forgiveness, salvation).

5. Good rulers and government officials can bring about order in society and even see that the physical needs or their constituents are met, but they cannot offer eternal salvation. Only God can provide that.

6. God "cleaned the slate," as it were, when Jesus died on the cross. This forgiveness is ours simply by believing.

7. Death is a result of sin; it became a reality for people at the time of the fall, when Adam and Eve first sinned. We die to shed our sinful self, so we may arise to everlasting life in Christ. Death provides freedom for the believer.

Closing

Sing or pray together the hymn "Blest the Children of Our God." Then close with prayer, thanking God for making you His forever children.

Lesson 10

Return to the Lord (Hosea 14; Review of Hosea)

Before the Session

This will be your last class session. Spend some time in evaluation. How has the study been received? Is there a close cohesiveness among class members? Is there a desire to continue to meet to study God's Word? You may want to discuss this during class time today and make arrangements to begin a new study.

Getting Started

As class members arrive, encourage them to work together to sum up what they have learned from Hosea. Have them find the original texts in Hosea that the New Testament quotes in these passages: **Matt. 2:15 [Hosea 11:1]; Matt. 9:13 [Hosea 6:6]; Matt. 12:7 [Hosea 6:6]; Luke 21:22 [Hosea 9:7]; Luke 23:30 [Hosea 10:8]; Rom. 9:25–26 [Hosea 2:23; 1:10]; 1 Cor. 15:54–55 [Hosea 13:14]; 2 Cor. 9:6 [Hosea 10:12]; Heb. 13:15 [Hosea 14:2]; 1 Peter 2:10 [Hosea 1:9–10]; Rev. 3:17 [Hosea 12:8].**

The Class Session

Open with prayer, preferably by a volunteer class member. Then have another member read the "Goal" and "What's Going On Here?" sections. Encourage questions and discussion about these sections.

Searching the Scriptures

A Plea and a Pledge (Hosea 14)

1. The people were to confess their sinfulness and ask for forgiveness. Our faith is shown through the fruit we bear: love, joy, peace, patience, kindness, goodness, faithfulness, gentleness, and self-control. We offer to God the fruit of our lips—praise.

2. The Israelites were to throw out all their man-made and man-appointed idols and make known their belief in the one true God. Likewise, that is our mandate.

3. If Israel will return to Him, the Lord's anger will turn to healing and forgiving love. God does this because of the redeeming act of His beloved Son, Jesus. Hosea describes God's blessings as refreshing dew, a beautiful lily blossom, a strong and fragrant cedar, a fruitful olive tree and grain field, a protective tree, a blossoming vine, and a well-known fine wine. If time permits, linger awhile over these expressions and challenge the class members to make up a few of their own.

4. Wisdom comes from learning and taking to heart God's holy Word. We walk in God's ways when we follow His commands and live as Jesus lived. Enabled by God, we are motivated to do this out of thanks for the free gift of forgiveness and eternal life purchased with the blood of Christ on the cross.

Hosea's Prophecy in Review

1. Hosea poured out his love to Gomer, only to be put down, ridiculed, used, and abused. Abraham was to sacrifice his only son, the son of God's promise. Moses was to leave a comfortable life to carry out the difficult task of leading God's people out of their slavery. Paul would give up the life he had known and be persecuted for the faith for which he had once persecuted others. We respond like these men, who put their fears and trepidation into God's hands and stepped out in faith to do as He had commanded. We do this empowered by the Holy Spirit working through God's Word to strengthen our faith.

2. The unity in the testimonies comes from the single source of inspiration of the prophets—God's Holy Spirit.

3. Class members will probably cite most of the book of Hosea! God could not have been more clear in his call for repentance.